ENDOR

I wish this book had been available when I was leading operational CEO roles during my career, as I knew many logical and task-oriented individuals that would have greatly benefited from its wisdom.

Anne explains soft skills in simple terms with very practical advice and tools to change their behaviour and have better results.

Full of tips, challenges, client stories and personal anecdotes, the book provides practical ideas to get better results through better engagement with others.

The higher you go in an organization, the more important people skills become, and this book is a good primer for improving your proficiency and satisfaction around working with others.

An easy read, simply explained and direct, with lots of practical tips and tools to become a more collaborative leader for greater impact. A great starter to help any manager understand their impact, intentionally create better relationships and be more effective in their job to deliver the results. I strongly recommend it.

> Nandu (Doreswamy) Nandkishore, Former Global CEO Nestlé Nutrition & EVP (CEO) of Asia/Oceania/Africa for Nestle S.A. Now a Keynote speaker/VC/consultant/B-school Prof

Anne has truly upped the game in the people development world. She has brilliantly brought together many dimensions of the soft skill tool bag and made them easy to understand and applicable to our daily lives. And dare I say this is so needed in our "fast paced get ahead at all cost" world. Thank you, Anne!

If you want people in your world to feel deeply valued and supported ... this is a must read!

> Rick Tamlyn, Hay House Author – *Play Your Bigger Game*, and Co-Active Training Institute Senior Faculty Member

Soft Skills Hard Results is an easy to understand and comprehensive book, loaded with practical tips and techniques that the reader can immediately apply and benefit from. It saves leaders – who want to improve their self-awareness and/or relationship skills – from reading 10+ different books and having to decode their terminology.

Anne has compiled 360 degrees of information – from neuroscience to emotional intelligence to coaching – and enriched it with sound personal experience coming from both her private life and a successful career.

I would definitely recommend this book to all leaders who want to be in a journey to a better self, whilst getting great business results!

Nilgün Kuruöz, Professional Coach and Consultant, Nilsight

This book on leadership based on the narration of Anne's life story is told in a simple yet gripping and powerful way and relates to our everyday lives – both professional and private. Having worked with Anne over the years I can attest to the effectiveness and efficiency of her methods and approach. She ensures that both aspects of leading with your head and heart are fully explored.

If you truly wish to make a lasting positive impact and change on people's lives (and your own) – this is a must-read book which is hands on and truly "a practical guide to understanding and using people skills for hard results".

Washington Munetsi, HR Director Operations Nestlé

Anne Taylor has been one of my "go-to" coaches, who I can turn to without hesitation to step in and counsel individuals or teams that need to re-examine their leadership style as an essential element of successful execution on innovative ideas. I have long admired her work and marvelled at her results.

In *Soft Skills Hard Results*, she reveals the logic that has guided her success and it is an intelligent, informative and valuable read. The book integrates different approaches to analysing leadership performance in a search for success and provides vivid illustrations of how these speak to the art of leadership in a variety of organizational settings.

I recommend this book to anyone looking to become more effective in a leadership role no matter what the context.

Bill Fischer, Professor of Innovation Management, IMD, Lausanne, Switzerland

The foundation of most careers is built on expertise and problem-solving abilities – the hard skills that produce results and manage complexity.

In *Soft Skills Hard Results*, Anne provides a roadmap for analytical leaders to connect with the needs of their teams and how to create an environment where their team can work together to be successful – to take risks, share responsibility and deliver results. Drawing on her years of experience as a coach, Anne lays out how with reflection and simple, practical exercises you can, as a leader, develop your natural style to connect and engage with your team.

Anne's practical guide not only produces results but makes the experience of achieving your goals and objectives more rewarding than you could have ever expected.

Sean Westcott, Head, Nestlé Product
Technology Centre Food (Culinary) at Nestlé

More than worth your time to read! It's so simple and easy to digest, in part because of the clear layout of the material. This is a really useful "handbook" especially for new managers/leaders or those wanting more insight and every day, real-world tools.

I really do like the simplicity of the concepts, and the challenges that Anne offers which include great questions to ask yourself and those with whom you work. She has outlined 10 Practical Principles that the reader needs to actually try to bring the results to life. Anne has split the book into 4 Parts – Inside (self), Outside (others), Between (our relationships) and Beyond (the future) which creates real clarity of how leaders need to work on themselves first (inside) within the bigger picture of the legacy they want to create (the future).

It's also a good companion book for a manager or leader who wants coaching or who is just starting to be coached. It gives practical things to do that then can be further explored during the coaching.

Soft Skills Hard Results is a practical, simple book that is easy to connect with. It comes alive, as through sharing her personal experiences, Anne demonstrates the vulnerability that managers and leaders need and that makes the book really different.

Hilary Oliver PCC, Leadership Coach, Coach Trainer &
Supervisor and 2017 ICF Global Chair

I highly recommend and endorse *Soft Skills Hard Results* by Anne Taylor. Anne was my executive coach and she was practical in her approach, deliberate and introduced me to soft skills (emotional intelligence). She helped me to understand the value of working on improving my people skills (or soft skills) in and outside the workplace which helped me to continue to deliver results and improved my relationship with my team whilst improving the culture.

For me, this was the missing link in what would be future success both at work and outside the workplace. Anne brings the same practical examples and lessons to this book. With this book you'll progress through 10 Principles of soft skills presented in 4 Parts. Anne uses lists, bullet points, tips, cases, illustrations and frameworks so you spend less time reading prose-dense pages and more time actually putting the skills into practice.

For those leaders who are looking to deliver results while building a strong culture, collaborative environment and emotionally intelligent team, I highly recommend you get this book.

Dan Persad, Global Banking (Strategy & Execution)

Sr Executive

A Practical Guide to
People Skills for
Analytical Leaders

soft
skills **HARD**
RESULTS

ANNE TAYLOR

First published in Great Britain by Practical Inspiration Publishing, 2020

ISBN   978-1-78860-139-9 (print)
           978-1-78860-137-5 (mobi)
           978-1-78860-138-2 (epub)

Back cover photography by Darius Bashar

Contents

Note To Reader

Why You?

You care about results. You get things done. You are successful. You lead with your head (rational, analytical and logical). You're an analytical leader. That has worked up to now. The world and business are changing, at an accelerated rate, and will continue to be uncertain and complex.

You feel you *should*, or you have been *told* to, engage, motivate and inspire your teams more. Or maybe you genuinely want to engage them more. This means you recognize that you would benefit from leading more from your heart (emotional, collaborative, and vulnerable). And now you're ready to tackle that, effectively and efficiently.

Regardless of where you are in the hierarchy of the organization, you are a leader. Leaders are not just defined by their position or title in the organization. They are defined by the impact they have on others in pursuit of achieving the goals.

Why Now?

Your organization and, by extension, you, face an exhausting list of challenges that demand a different way of leading:

- Rising intergenerational differences with millennials and Gen-Zs in the workforce

- Increasing stress and emotions of and among staff

- Setting yourself apart from your peers

- Escalating speed and uncertainty of technology, competition, regulation and consumer needs and wants

- Trying to achieve more with less

- Addressing feedback that you could be warmer, more people-oriented or more inspiring

- Increasing confidence, competence and empathy in your interpersonal interactions

Quite simply, soft skills can address all these challenges. The Practical Principles in this book, when applied, practised and honed, can improve your effectiveness, impact and results. They can help you manage those with whom you work in the context of a business environment in which decisions need to be nuanced, certainty has been replaced with ambiguity or simply unrelenting change.

Soft skills are people skills (as opposed to hard or technical skills like accountancy, building a house, assembling a manufacturing line, merchandising a product display in a retail store). If you are running a project to build a piece of infrastructure or design a new car, you'll need hard skills: engineering, planning, cost-estimating, scheduling. These are the skills that will enable delivery of some kind of output. Yet the skills associated with whether what you produce is successful are largely soft: working with the client or managing your supply chain; negotiating changes to the scope of the project; agreeing solutions to address unanticipated risk; managing any conflict; keeping everyone committed to the project.

They are the behaviours we use when interacting with other people. You might not think of them as skills though (yet). You might feel they are just what you do to communicate and relate with others, be it your family, friends or work colleagues.

Let's work through an example: An experienced project manager (PM) was asked by her Director to move from leading a new product development team to leading a process improvement team instead, because it would be better for the company. The PM said she'd think about it and commented that she would have less profile with the new project and occasionally have to travel further as many team members were at a different site. The Director blurted out: "Fine. Don't do it. We have someone else who can lead it." And with that she turned and walked away, leaving the project manager feeling taken for granted and that she'd annoyed the Director. She would have preferred that the Director acknowledge the inconvenience and status change, even if it wasn't possible to compensate her for it, and that "they'd appreciate her doing it for the company anyway". It would have taken no more time or effort to have acknowledged the issue and shown appreciation that she was doing the company a favour. The PM would have felt valued and the Director wouldn't have had to spend time reaching out to another PM.

Miscommunication and poor people skills left both the PM and her Director irritated with a less than good solution.

What you say and how you say it will have an impact on the other person and the result you get. What you say and how you say it are influenced by who you are, your personality and preferences, and how you feel. If you behave in a skilful way when interacting with others you will create the impact you want and improve the likelihood of getting the result you want. The good news – these skills can be learned, practised and mastered. The great news – science says people skills or emotional intelligence, which is the broader domain that is explained below, can be grown or developed.[1]

Soft skills aren't fluffy. The cost of underdeveloped people skills is inefficiency and lost productivity. Conversely, the upside is increased productivity, engagement and often satisfaction. This book will help you balance your head-smart strengths through simple tools, frameworks and exercises challenging you to become more heart-smart for the benefit of the business, your team and yourself (even if that doesn't interest you at this moment).

Soft skills have their roots in Emotional Intelligence or EI (sometimes called EQ to complement IQ). EI is the overarching term to describe four concepts: the ability to know one's emotions, manage one's emotions, understand the emotions of other people, and manage relationships with others. As the *English Oxford Living Dictionary* defines it: "the capacity to be aware of, control, and express one's emotions, and to handle interpersonal relationships judiciously and empathetically". The concept was popularized in the

1996 book *Emotional Intelligence* by Daniel Goleman, still a great reference to this day.[2] The four areas of EI are illustrated below.

EI: EMOTIONAL INTELLIGENCE		
	SELF	OTHER
KNOWING	**Self-Awareness** Knowing one's emotions	**Social Awareness** Recognizing emotions in others
DOING	**Self-Management** Managing one's emotions Motivating oneself	**Social Management** Handling relationships, interactions with others

Knowing on its own isn't enough to have great emotional intelligence. You must risk putting it into practice daily to be great at it. *Soft Skills* Hard Results will touch on all four aspects of EI to the extent necessary for you to benefit and see results while still being able to do your day job.

Why This Book?

Soft Skills Hard Results is a practical guide to understanding and using people skills (or soft skills) in the workplace (and outside work if you want). It might be a precursor to studying emotional intelligence in the future, or not (for you to decide when you finish reading and implementing).

With this book you'll progress through 10 Principles of soft skills presented in 4 Parts. It's designed to be as practical as possible, for maximum understanding and application in minimal reading time. I use lists, bullet points, tips, cases, illustrations and frameworks so you spend less time reading prose-dense pages and more time actually putting the skills into practice.

The Introduction illustrates the importance of soft skills to business and bottom-line results. It will help you internalize why emotions matter and why soft skills and human interactions are crucial to success. Very often your career advancement and business results are determined more by how you do what you do, rather than just the tasks you get done – this is especially true the higher in the organization you climb.

Part 1 is called *Inside* as it starts with you, knowing yourself as a person and what leadership is about for you. You'll assemble all the things you already know about yourself such as your personality and skills. You'll also learn some new things about yourself such as your values and the 'stories' you hold in your head about yourself. The idea is you should have a holistic and somewhat objective view of yourself. Every single human relationship you have has one thing in common – YOU!

Part 2 is called *Outside* as it's about impacting (positively) the people with whom you interact and work. It's about putting the emphasis on others for their benefit (and ultimately your benefit, hence getting the needed results). You'll learn about giving feedback, why and how to coach, and the 'what and how' of storytelling – very practical steps to make it easy and effective.

Part 3 is called *Between* as it's the dance or interaction between the two; the inside and the outside, you and others. How to be yourself ('authentically you' in self-help jargon) while allowing other people to be themselves and still get things done. It's about balance – within you and towards others. This Part may be challenging for you, and I ask that you persist; it can transform your leadership if you let it.

Part 4 is called *Beyond* as it's about enjoying the journey; it transcends the specific actions and tasks. When I was writing this book the Part 4 material started as a bonus chapter and grew in importance to become a full Part in its own right. Don't worry, there is practical advice included and, in some respects, this might be the start of the journey for you rather than the end of this book. It's what started me on this work as an Executive Coach and, quite frankly, what started me on my development as a more balanced head-smart and heart-smart human being. It's about living a life of gratitude and no regrets – with simple exercises to put this into practice. I'd hate for you to retire and look back wondering "What if? What more?"

There are no revolutionary new ideas in this book, rather a new way to understand and apply the Principles which you probably are already familiar with. I'll focus on the key people skills that have big impact, with each Principle ending in a challenge for you to implement immediately. By taking on the challenges you will improve your everyday working life so that over time you will increase your confidence in navigating the emotional aspects at work. **In essence, user-friendly tips and tricks of essential people skills for business with immediate application potential to deliver bottom-line results and long-term fulfilment.**

Why Me?

I was raised in part by a businessman, educated in business, I worked in business across many regions and countries for big multinationals, and I am still exposed to business through clients and academia. Now I run my own successful solopreneur business having coached hundreds if not thousands in business in the UK and abroad. *All of that means business is at my core.* The surprising deaths of both my parents close together, the end of my 26-year relationship, and moving to a country where I knew only three people introduced me to the world of emotional vulnerability *which has grown my heart.* I've learned how leveraging both the head and heart strengths positively affects leaders and their businesses and ultimately success and satisfaction.

I am the Director of Directions Coaching Ltd. Prior to this, armed with my degree in Business from Wilfrid Laurier University in Canada, I had over 20 years of business experience at companies such as IBM, Procter & Gamble and Nestlé where I held positions of increasing responsibility in marketing, overall business management and business strategy development.

After leaving my Global Marketing role at Nestlé in Switzerland following my parents' deaths, I retrained as an Executive Coach. My first clients included IMD (Institute for Management Development) business school and Nestlé. Later, in the UK, I established a successful practice with clients such as LEGO®, Deutsche Bank, L'Oréal and Ford among others, as well as a collection of personal clients investing in themselves. I am an associate coach for London Business School and LHH Penna. I am certified through the ICF (International Coach Federation) to the level of PCC (Professional Certified Coach – one of a small number in the UK).

As a recent client said after our first session, "that was comfortably uncomfortable". As an Executive Coach, I create safe places for executives to grow as leaders and, dare I say, human beings (even if that's not relevant to them initially). Through a structured process that includes observations, intuition and reflection, they increase their self-awareness to make more conscious choices. I bring challenge & support, directness & tenderness, provocation & acceptance, and head & heart to clients. All in service of them identifying their goals, removing barriers, questioning assumptions and beliefs, and practising new behaviours, to create lasting change that they want for themselves.

My Wish for You

In today's world of technology, I feel we are losing real human connection that facilitates work getting done well and our sense of satisfaction in what we do. That's what this book is about for me: connection – to self and others – in order to make a great contribution. My wish for you is that you try the challenges at the end of each Principle. Ideally, you should set aside time each week to do the challenge work and then practise, practise, practise. This is about practising the tips and frameworks presented here. It's going to feel uncomfortable and awkward, all things do at first. These simple Principles have the potential to transform your leadership (professionally and personally) and your fulfilment. Yes, people skills will improve your performance at work and help you achieve results. The

Consortium for Research on Emotional Intelligence in Organizations extensively documents "how emotional intelligence contributes to bottom line in any work organization".[3] I'm hoping the use of soft skills and the ensuing results will entice you to lead a life of personal development and psychologically healthy fulfilment – that powerful balance of head- and heart-smart.

I learned these skills later in my life, better late than never at least. They weren't overt growing up in my family, nor were they abundant at business school. I support my clients in learning and living these skills, first for their leadership and then for themselves. Both I and my clients experience more enjoyable and productive interactions. I don't know how to stress how much I want this for you! Visit my website (www. directions-coaching.com) for more information and ideas on this topic and about my 1:1 coaching services that support leaders on this journey. The notes and bibliography section of this book provide invaluable information in the broader leadership space.

Introduction:
Soft Skills Are Crucial To Work
(And Life) Success

This introduction will lay out the facts for why soft skills deliver hard results. It will do this by illustrating the tangible cost of poor people skills. It will explain the pivotal role and presence of emotions even at work, through factual neuroscience and brain anatomy. It will remind you that the make-or-break tasks in your company (and their associated measurements, key performance indicators – KPIs) can be made or broken by good or bad soft skills respectively. The financials and biology in this section *might be helpful and of interest* to some to 'prove' the importance of you proceeding with the work in this book. For others, it might not be necessary. *You decide how much you need to digest in this introduction to understand how crucial soft skills are.*

People skills are about balancing the head-smart with the heart-smart, or leveraging one's EI more to complement IQ. To be clear, EI does not replace IQ, abilities, hard skills and capabilities. Organizations need to ensure their people are trained to the necessary level to perform their job. By becoming more skilled in soft skills, your organization will:

- Improve employee engagement and retention

- Generate innovative ideas (almost every corporation lists innovation in its mission)

- Foster an open, collaborative working environment

- And hence improve productivity and bottom-line results[1]

The Tangible Cost of Soft Skills

Imagine you have a manager who is in an open-plan office criticizing one of their employees for five minutes. How long do you think that employee is demotivated or unproductive? How long do you think the others in the office are unproductive (trying to console the berated employee or criticizing the manager's action)? Imagine this manager does this every day to one person. This can cost thousands of pounds, euros, dollars!

I recently did the maths for a leader of a small, family-owned enterprise, with him providing the numbers and me just doing the calculation. I called it monetizing soft skills – figuring out the monetary value of a leader's people skills. Their supply chain manager was complaining and criticizing people (in their own team) on a daily basis. The leader was reluctant to act because he wasn't comfortable giving constructive feedback, so convinced himself that it wouldn't make a difference, it wasn't that big a deal, and ultimately, he was avoiding what he thought would be conflict (I hear this fear and avoidance from so many leaders in small and large organizations).

Monetizing Soft Skills

How often does she do this a day?	4x day
How many days per week does she do this?	5x week (daily)
How many people in the office?	15 people
How long do you think those 15 people are thrown off by the negativity	5 min each
How many weeks per year does she do this? (ex. vacation)	46 weeks
So for 15 people losing 5 minutes each, 4x per day, 5 days/wk, 46 wks	69,000min/yr lost
Average salary of the employees in that space	$/£/€50,000 yr or $/£/€0.401/min
Let's be conservative and divide the impact in half	- 50%
Lost productivity ($/£/€0.401/minute x 69,000 minutes x 50%)	$/£/€13,834yr

This example illustrates the tangible productivity loss of one manager in a small office exhibiting poor people skills. If you could add $/£/€14,000 to your bottom-line would it be worth having a conversation with the supply chain manager? Take it a step further and imagine how the gains in the team's time allowed them to take on more initiatives or better drive the strategy to long-term benefit.

I've done this for a leader in an office where each staff member is billed out at £120 per hour, and the calculation resulted in over £60,000 of lost productivity.

That leader had the conversation; the numbers forced it. The manager ended up leaving of his own accord, and the new manager is loved and billable hours have increased.

This example quantifies the tangible cost of poor people skills. It does not quantify the increase in productivity of good or excellent people skills. The calculation could be done for positive skills when people are inspired or routinely motivated; it's just harder to do, it feels more subjective. There's a positive upside for soft skills too – imagine the impact on productivity of an individual or team when you acknowledge someone's strong contribution.

The incidences of a berating manager are few for my clients. The incidences of empathetic and inspiring managers are few for my clients. Most managers fall in the middle, into the category of simply not knowing how to engage and motivate their teams. The big opportunity to positively add to the bottom-line is not the critical manager, instead it's *the managers who simply do nothing* because they don't know what to do.

In the above berating example most of the lost productivity can be traced to the team members who had been thrown off by the manager's negativity. You can't deny that when a manager criticizes an employee in public, other people get concerned, they're afraid they will be shamed next, they second-guess their performance and worry. Often in these situations employees will later sympathize with the 'victim or target' of the criticism at the coffee station, saying how it was undeserved or the manager just doing their usual rant. Again, this is time of lost productivity. This is an example of how emotions can influence the workplace and hence results. When you think of these types of situations happening in most offices on a daily basis you can't deny emotions are present at work, it's not all facts and objectivity. The next section will explain the brain structure (facts to justify the data) and the presence of emotions in humans (including employees!).

Humans: Emotional Beings Capable of Incredible Things

We are human beings, an interconnection of thoughts, feelings and physicality. Humans are emotionally driven even in business, despite how much we want to say, "business is rational and factual". The reason for this is that humans are complex beings of physical, energetic and chemical systems that create our experience of life. Add time (be it human evolution or our personal time on earth) to that, and the complexity increases.

1. Evolution of the Brain

Technology is not the only change going on; humans continue to evolve. Evolution does not necessarily mean we get better, it means we adapt better to our environment. Our brains continue to evolve and as a result have both primitive and advanced elements. The brain can be divided into three basic parts:

- Reptilian (as this part is found in reptiles too) – this is the primitive part, focused exclusively on survival, it does not think, it reacts, this is where the pre-programmed responses of fight, flight and freeze reside.

- Limbic system (shared with other mammals) – this is the centre for emotions, memories, feelings and motivations. The amygdala is a small segment of the brain located here. When we are at the mercy of the fight or flight response from the reptilian brain or intense emotions from the limbic system, Daniel Goleman refers to this as an "amygdala hijack".[2] In an amygdala hijack we react on autopilot unless the neocortex intervenes.

- Neocortex – this is our processor, this is where we process abstract thought, logic, and words. It's this area of the brain that can override the emotions of the other two parts of the brain. This is the place of choice. We choose the meaning we give to a person, thing, situation or anything really. Imagine you're on a hike and you see a long, dark, slender, cylindrical object. Is it a snake, a stick or a piece of tube (because the path you're walking on backs onto a plumber's yard)? That type of processing of external stimuli happens in the neocortex.

The neocortex consists of the left hemisphere and right hemisphere. We use both parts of our brains; however, many people experience through their upbringing a predisposition to one side.[3]

- Right hemisphere – freedom, open, broader focus, alertness, intuition, newness, pictures, learns by body movement, a parallel processor, the present moment, part of a bigger whole.

People characterized as right-brained might prefer charts and pictures in their reports; discuss the bigger context of a project and might get bored with some of the details; probably enjoy brainstorming sessions; go with their gut-feel on decisions more often; when organizing their office they focus on a categorization system for future organizing; they will be quite expressive in their communication; they may suggest music for an away-day and talk of how things fit together in the bigger picture. They probably focus on the feelings amongst colleagues rather than the specific behaviours. They might prefer occupations like marketing and advertising.

- Left hemisphere – narrow focus, attention to detail, language, reason, logic, structure, analysis, linear orientation, a serial processor, the past and the future, the voice in your head.

People characterized as left-brained might prefer numbers, facts and data in their reports; adhere to critical paths and project details; rely on logic and weigh pros and cons when making decisions; when organizing their files they focus on the individual files; they may be direct and straightforward in their communication; they may adhere to meeting agendas and go through them in an orderly fashion; they will analyze something rather than sense how they feel about it. They might prefer occupations like engineering or accounting.

The Human Brain

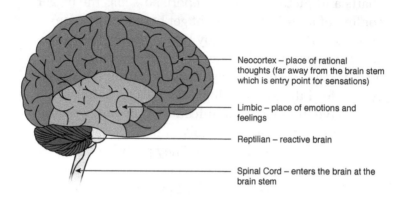

Neocortex – place of rational thoughts (far away from the brain stem which is entry point for sensations)

Limbic – place of emotions and feelings

Reptilian – reactive brain

Spinal Cord – enters the brain at the brain stem

Information from our five senses (touch, taste, sight, sound and smell) is transmitted through our nervous system to the brain via the brain stem. The brain stem is located at the back of the brain which means that nerve sensations physically hit the emotional space of the brain, the limbic system, **first** before getting to the higher reasoning part of the brain near the forehead. It's the communication between these two parts of our brain that is the physical source of emotional intelligence according to Travis Bradberry and Jean Greaves in *The Emotional Intelligence Quick Book*.[4]

The emotional part of our brain is stimulated first, before the executive functioning or reasoning part of our brain! Hence, emotions are always present first when we take in stimuli – this means that even at work our brain structure and its evolution prove emotions are ever present. More later on about whether we display or act on that emotion, whether we react from that emotion, how we convey that initial emotional impulse or not.

2. Neuroscience

Another effect on our experiences in work (and life) is the system of chemicals operating unconsciously in our bodies. Neuroscience, the study of the brain and nervous system, has made significant strides in understanding the brain, the interconnectedness of the systems and the impact of the chemicals on our minds and bodies. *Psychology Today* describes it as the intersection of psychology and biology to further our understanding of physical, psychological and neurological health conditions. My focus is on neuroscience as it relates to coaching as this is about maximizing our potential (and the potential of your employees). Specifically, how our internal systems, especially body chemistry, influence our reactions in daily life, and the concept of neuroplasticity, our brain's ability to learn. Let me explain some key terms.

Adrenalin – a hormone secreted by the adrenal glands that increases circulation, breathing and prepares the body physically for exertion (like running – be it in a race or from a lion).

Cortisol – a hormone released during times of stress; it activates the bodily functions associated with short-term survival and as such depresses the immune system. It works with epinephrine (adrenalin) to create memories of short-term emotional events (to remember what to avoid in the future).

Dopamine – a chemical released by nerve cells which is responsible for reward-driven learning; every type of reward increases dopamine transmission to the brain. It enables us to see rewards and make actions towards them.

Neuroplasticity – the capacity of the nervous system including the brain to change well into adulthood, such as cellular changes due to learning. In other words, our brains can form new neural pathways even as we age. Myth busting – you can teach an old dog new tricks, if they want to learn and go about it consistently.

Norepinephrine – the second neurotransmitter (besides dopamine) that stabilizes the prefrontal cortex (the very front part of the neocortex). At moderate amounts it leads to feelings of alertness and paying close attention. At too high a level it actually decreases mental acuity.

Oxytocin – acts as a neurotransmitter to reduce the stress hormone cortisol and facilitate bonding. It evokes feelings of contentment, reductions in anxiety and feelings of calmness and security around another person. Studies show a correlation between oxytocin and human bonding.

Seratonin – 90% is located in the gut; it regulates learning, memory, mood, sleep and constriction of the blood vessels.

So, what we're learning from neuroscience as applied to human potential is that a certain amount of stress is worthwhile to motivate us to pursue goals, and too much stress or fear impedes us. Fear or an amygdala hijack means our reptilian brain is taking over, our executive functioning is not in control, our brain is less integrated (not using all three parts/both hemispheres), and we are reacting. Adrenalin and cortisol are released, our breathing rate increases, circulation increases, we are less connected to our bodies. When we are cared for and valued, oxytocin is released, anti-inflammatory hormones are present, both of which result in us having access to all parts of our brain. We are then able to respond not react, able to consciously make choices, able to tap into our bodies and intuition and hence contribute more positively.

Neuroplasticity is the term describing the newfound fact that our brains can create new neural pathways. Historically it was thought that as we age we no longer create new neural pathways in our brain – summed up by 'you can't teach an old dog new tricks'. Now science has proven that we can create new neural pathways if we practise new thoughts and behaviours that allow us to respond in new ways that better serve us. We can re-program our mind in essence to handle stressful or scary situations in a more proactive, intentional way. For example, when having to make a presentation to a large audience you can plan and practise different behaviours and thoughts to encourage pleasure rather than fear. For example, think of what success would be, imagine a time you were confident in the past and apply it as you rehearse, have a ritual just before starting the presentation that reminds you of your positivity about the occasion, use lots of sensory inputs when rehearsing and presenting (touch the lectern, smell the odours in the room, hear the sounds, intentionally plan the physicality of your body on the stage). Research shows adults only strengthen new neural pathways (physically it's a thicker layer of myelin coating the outside of the nerve, insulating it in effect for faster habitual response) by doing, practising, and experimenting, whereas children can strengthen the pathways by both doing and just thinking new things (oh, the ease is lost on the young!).[5]

3. Social Creatures

Humans are herd animals. Some sociologists say humans were herd animals and are now social animals. Regardless of the exact label, humans survive only in highly coordinated groups.[6] In fact, being part of a group is so important to humans that we conform, often unconsciously.

A work team is a distinct herd or social group. Employees want to feel as if they belong to that group. To belong and be part of a social group it is imperative to skilfully navigate human interactions or relationships. We just want to belong and feel welcome and part of a collective, and since we spend so much time at work it is important to create this feeling for your teams.

Leadership Is about Relationships

Most problems in work situations are a result of human interactions rather than work tasks. That might sound like a bold statement; however, take a moment and reflect on this. Think of the times in your career that have been fulfilling, that felt easy and seemed to be less stressful. Often, they will be the times when the relationships were working well, when you enjoyed the people you were working with and there were few 'difficult interactions or characters'.

Most people quit their job because of a manager rather than an organization, as Forbes noted in 2015: "people leave managers not companies".[7] That means the relationship with the manager is pivotal to someone's longevity within an organization, moreso than the company values, the work they perform or the output of the company.

As managers move up in an organization and get promoted to increasing levels of responsibility, their jobs change and the skills required change. I have often worked with technical leaders who were great workers and then they got promoted. They no longer coded or programmed or ran experiments or designed machinery; rather they dealt with people who were doing that more hands-on work. They became removed from the day-to-day tasks and started overseeing others doing those tasks they once loved. As they continued to get promoted they were distanced from the work and skills they had developed and soon dealt with managers overseeing the workers. Their responsibilities became about setting the goals and supporting and facilitating others to achieve those goals. The work of a leader becomes influencing, supporting, inspiring, clearing barriers and navigating organizational structures and differing priorities, which is all about relationships and people.

Your Company Results Rely on Soft Skills

As you know, the financial structure or model of most organizations, in a simplified explanation, is top-line income or revenue, minus the expenses of running the organization, resulting in the remaining profit.

Basic Business or Organizational Financial Model

+ Income
− Expenses
= Profit

The difficult thing to see within that model and on a profit and loss statement is that each line on that P&L can be impacted by soft skills. For the income, revenue or top-line sales, the link to people skills is quite evident, whether it's an organization that sells products or services or a fund-raising enterprise securing donations – successful sales people or fund-raisers often have excellent people skills. They are curious to understand their customers' needs and feelings and then position how their company's product meets those needs. When a sales person understands their product well, understands their customers' needs thoroughly, and then illustrates the mutual benefit to the customer (remember win-win from years ago?), they have done their job and progressed towards meeting their sales target and hence generated income for the company. Sales people cannot have poor interactions with their customers while still achieving sustainable revenues.

The importance of soft skills and relationships is the same for the 'expense' portion of the business as it is for the 'revenue' portion. When a company has good relationships with its customers/consumers, labour force and suppliers, it often benefits – both tangibly and intangibly. When business interactions are consistently conducted with positive people skills, business moves from being transactional in nature to being more relationship-led. Let's start with the most obvious example of people skills impacting the P&L, which is customer service departments. When a customer has a complaint about your organization's product or service they are encouraged (by good companies) to contact the customer service department to get it rectified. A good customer service representative will use excellent soft skills to address the customer's complaint. Another example is labour or the human resource cost on the P&L. An employee who feels valued and engaged is less likely to quit, saving recruitment costs, and less likely to demand extreme compensation (assuming their basic need is met). The people skills that lead to staff feeling involved keep salary expenses within reason and reduce absenteeism thereby contributing to productivity more consistently. Another cost of goods example is supplier relationships. Good relations that use positive people skills with a supplier can result in discounts, advantageous payment terms, quicker exposure to new initiatives, and sharing ideas that could benefit the business.

Each Principle in this book, including this introduction, will include a challenge for you to complete at the end of the description. The challenge is meant to spur you into action by identifying skills to practise and lessons to learn through self-reflection. It's the type of challenge I give my executive clients in 1:1 coaching. I challenge them to try new things between coaching sessions and then reflect on what works and what doesn't. The words in this book will not improve your performance nor your company's performance. Only your action will improve the bottom-line. Thinking about something doesn't make the improvement, acting on it does. I suggest you get a blank journal or notebook and use it as you progress through this book, so you capture everything in one place and can revisit things as you learn more.

THE CHALLENGE

The purpose of this challenge is to notice the importance of soft skills in business (everywhere in fact). Where are things working for you and for your team and for the organization? And where could they be better? What value would positive people skills have on your business' bottom-line?

On a scale of 1–10, where 1 is not at all effective and 10 is highly effective, where would you place yourself on how skilfully and consistently you use soft skills at work?

Where could your organization's bottom-line be improved with better people skills or better relationships?

Which of your relationships could improve – either negative to better, or good to great?

Where would more engagement and innovation benefit the business?

What's the mood or energy in your workplace? Is it fear oriented, neutral, or growth and learning oriented?

What's your belief about the importance of soft skills in business?

Spend one hour this week doing the exercise above. What are the themes or patterns or beliefs that emerge for you?

From your reflections, write down a minimum of five learnings or observations about yourself and five about your organization relative to soft skills and their importance. Identify five opportunities for leveraging the information in this introduction about soft skills – this means actions you can take directly and/or ways to influence others as needed.

Reflect on the exercise and topic:

▶ What did you learn about yourself from your reflections?

▶ What did you learn about other people from reflecting on these questions? Who does soft skills well?

▶ What would you like to celebrate around soft skills in the organization?

▶ Where in your organization would the most benefit be realized if there was a focus on soft skills?

PART 1

INSIDE

You need to understand the emotional realm of your employees and the work environment (or so you've been told) and that starts with understanding YOURSELF first – reflecting on you, not necessarily something you are used to or familiar with and probably not within your comfort zone. Don't worry; there will be clear questions and practical exploration, not just airy-fairy blah blah blah.

The INSIDE section is about putting the focus on yourself; understanding everything you know about you and then reflecting on it to identify who you are at your core and hence what you bring to the world (and to those with whom you interact). You can't realistically head to a destination, like Switzerland, without knowing that you are starting that trip from London or Toronto. Just like at work you can't hit the sales target for the year if you don't know the current sales figures. Self-awareness is a fundamental baseline if you are going to develop your skills.

By the end of Part 1 you will have accumulated and consolidated a variety of observations about you, both from your own perspective and from the perspectives of others. Your starting point will be the things you already know about yourself or have been told by others; this is the low-hanging fruit. If you've been on any leadership development or training courses, you'll probably have assessments and learning outcomes which you can reference. Once you've done that, I will help you go beyond the known or obvious, to explore the new and unknown and help you uncover motivators, preferences and aspects of yourself of which you may not currently be aware.

Having kicked off your inventory about yourself then you will investigate the SO WHAT? How do you manage yourself knowing what you now know in order to live the life you want; have the impact you intend and get the results to which you aspire? Does that sound lofty? If implemented it can help you manage yourself to influence key stakeholders at work, appropriately and effectively. Your day-to-day actions will be more about creating the life you want through conscious choice rather than happenstance. This process is similar to the kind of SWOT analysis you might undertake in your business to help you know your company's strengths and weaknesses and leverage them effectively to achieve the desired improvement and position in the marketplace.

Hope I have for you: This self-examination is a starting point for self-awareness. You may continue expanding your self-awareness well after finishing this book. We evolve and grow throughout our lives, so can always notice, learn and develop new things. And as you make conscious choices and notice the impact you are having on others you'll get further insight about yourself – but that's jumping ahead. On the other hand, if you so choose, your self-awareness journey may end with Part 1 – not because there's no further opportunity to learn, far from it, rather because you're not particularly interested in pursuing it further. I hope it's the former rather than the latter, as a life of periodic self-reflection (not constant navel-gazing) is richer and often more effective in achieving the results you want.

PRINCIPLE 1

It Starts With You

Improved people skills and, by extension, leadership, starts with you because <u>you</u> are the only person <u>you</u> can change. I'm sure you've tried changing other people, such as your partner or boss. How did that go? You may have been lucky if they changed at all. The greatest opportunity for change lies in knowing yourself well and focusing on what's within your control.

A tangential side diversion: that last sentence might have been awkward or felt unusual for you when reading it. That's because I used the word 'and' rather than the word 'but' which is customary in social language. I consciously chose 'and' because when 'but' is used in a sentence in our minds it often negates everything that comes before it. Whereas 'and' infers both sides of the sentence have merit or equal weight. Here's an example: "Your report was great, but the conclusion wasn't very memorable." What are you left to ponder? The poor conclusion. Conversely, "Your report was great, and the conclusion wasn't very memorable." Both parts of the sentence co-exist (you probably still feel the poor conclusion more because most achievement-oriented people are looking for something to do). Notice how often you use 'but' and try switching it to 'and'.

The starting point to people skills is to figure out your starting point. Who are you? A simple framework for what you are about to embark on is the Johari Window. It's a simple 2x2 model created by psychologists Joseph Luft and Harrington Ingham in 1955 and is useful for self-awareness and understanding relationships to others.

Johari Window

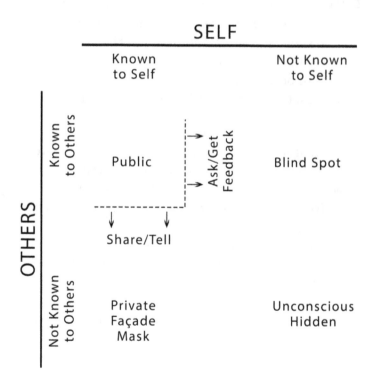

This Principle will be all about you – first, bringing what you already know about yourself to the forefront of your mind. This is the gather and collation phase.

Secondly, learning how to discover new insights about yourself or at least making some deeper things you know about yourself more conscious. This is the self-reflection and digging deeper phase. And finally, the Principle will end with a challenge to kickstart your understanding about your individuality and its impact on your effectiveness. This is the self-observation and curiosity phase.

Collate Existing Data about Yourself

Start by taking an inventory of all the available data you have on you. Look for all the evidence you have accumulated from recent years, including:

- Performance reviews

- 360^0 surveys (surveys that your boss, team and peers have completed on you)

- Awards and certifications

- Complaints or criticisms

- What are your passions? What do you enjoy doing?

- Any feedback you've received, e.g. verbal accolades, congratulatory cards, letters and emails

- Any assessments you've had done such as the Myers-Briggs Type Indicator (MBTI), DiSC Workplace Profile, Discovery Insights, The Leadership Circle, Hogan, Belbin Team Roles Assessment, Point Positive, Realize2 Strengths, Gallup Strengths Finder, Enneagram, etc. (If you don't have many of these types of assessment you can find some of them online with free or inexpensive versions to complete now)

- Comments from your friends and family (yes, really!)

If you don't have any of the above, then send a simple email to a variety of personal and professional contacts asking them for input. You can use the following verbatim to make it fast and easy for yourself, don't overthink it:

I am working on my leadership development (always a work in progress I feel) and would genuinely appreciate your input. Would you please respond to the following 4 questions with as much detail or specificity as you can (bearing in mind, your initial, quick response is best for both you and me):

1. *What should I start doing?*
2. *What should I stop doing?*
3. *What should I continue doing?*
4. *What is unique about me versus other leaders/people you know or with whom you work?*

Thank you so much for your feedback.

(As a bonus, the above model of start/stop/continue is a great way of asking for feedback. It gives people specific areas to think about rather than just 'how am I doing?' Or 'give me some feedback'. Keep to the start/stop/continue sequence as it makes it easier for the respondent to start the exercise and allows them to finish on a positive, so they don't feel bad.)

With regard to your friends and family, what comments would your partner or family members make about your strengths, weaknesses and that funny little quirk (potentially annoyance) that makes you distinctly you? What's the thing they tease you about? Extend that inquiry to your close friends, especially your best friend.

If the comments of your personal and professional contacts are similar, that is not surprising, as you are the same person at your core, just in two different environments. If the comments of personal and professional are radically different, what does that mean for you? What's happening inside you that leads to that distinction between your work and family personas?

From all the data/input above, start to classify the following:

- What are your strengths?

- What are your weaknesses?

- What makes you unique or distinct versus other individuals? Your company probably tries to differentiate itself from its competitors. This same differentiation is valuable to understand more about yourself as an individual. And you can use it later to differentiate yourself from your peers.

- What interests you most in life? In your work?

- What are your preferences for communicating? Decision making? Re-energizing? Perceiving the environment around you? Think of the type of people you enjoy working with most, and

chances are, they have similarities to you, so
that might help identify your preferences.

Take a stab at this summary; it doesn't have to be
perfect or 100% complete. Done is better than perfect
(as my book coach said before my first draft of this
book). This is a work-in-progress, just as you are. As
you go through the next phases you'll enhance this with
the new learnings you glean about yourself.

Harvest New Data – Personal and Professional Identity Narrative

Another great source of information can be gleaned
from a PPIN for yourself – Personal and Professional
Identity Narrative. Jack Wood, IMD Professor and
Jungian Analyst, encourages MBAs and Executives to
do this exercise for some of their greatest learning from
the program (a bold claim considering they were paying
tens of thousands of euros). The PPIN is your life story
– where you have come from, where you are right now
and the general trajectory of where you are headed or
where you think you might be headed. He says, "if you
take the PPIN seriously, the process of reflecting and
writing about your life – the sources of your identity
and the objectives that you embrace – can help you
better understand the deeper currents and patterns in
your life and their continued influence".[1]

Step 1 involves writing about the significant events in
your life. Just start. This is just a collection of small
stories, like chapters or simply paragraphs. You'll want
to cover your childhood (not just the facts, include
also your sense of what it was like growing up), school
experiences, work and career (it's not a CV/resumé
though), relationships (parental, romantic, friends),

what have been the highlights, the low points, the regrets (of what you've done or haven't done), the times of greatest learning and when things have felt effortless. Don't worry about whether it makes sense, is well written or in a logical format. This is only for you to read and analyze. Include examples, rich descriptions (not PowerPoint or bullet points) and your feelings and emotional reactions to the events and people.

I did the first draft of my PPIN in a week and ended up with over 10 typed pages, single spaced. Remember, I like to write and am a good typist, so I don't want to intimidate you. A couple of months later, it was in excess of 20 pages. Jack Wood suggests 5–10 pages for the first draft and 10–15 pages for the complete narrative. If done exhaustively it can take a while, so at worst, it's a legacy for your children (although it might be too revealing if done with no fear of it being seen). I'd encourage you to do more than what makes you comfortable; it's at the edges of our comfort zones where we learn the most and feel energized.

Step 2 is the analysis of what you've written. The informative part happens during the reflection. This might be while you are writing it or once it's written; when the patterns and themes in your life emerge (or appear once you observe your story on paper at a distance). What have you noticed about what you've created in your life? What's been easy? What's been hard? What has impacted you from one situation to another situation? What did you conclude about yourself or the way life works from the various events in your life? Where does it point you to in terms of further personal development? What patterns are influencing you?

For example, the PPIN exercise helped me understand why I adjusted so quickly when I moved from Canada to Switzerland; as a kid I had moved to a new city every five years due to my father's career. Prior to the first move my parents asked an education specialist for advice on moving young children. He told my parents to move my brother and me a month or two before the end of the school year as that would allow us to make friends before being let off school for the summer. That way we'd know other kids in the neighbourhood with whom to play. This meant that at the new school I was put into established classes with groups of children who had been together for months and, as the newbie, I was required to integrate. I remembered one situation in Grade 3 (so I was about 9 years old) where I was escorted into the classroom by a school secretary after the kids had already started their day. The room was a mixed group of both Grade 3s and 4s and I was stood at the front of the class and asked to introduce myself. I did this on more than one occasion. Hence when I arrived in Switzerland, I just threw myself in, introducing myself to strangers. The PPIN helped me recognize this pattern; understand that aspect of myself and become more conscious of using the skill when it served me (such as when I moved to England on my own and without a job).

Unearth Potential New Data – Values

What Are Values?

Most organizations and companies have values. You can usually find them listed on a company's website or in the induction materials as a new hire. Just as a company has values which help define it and how it operates, individuals do too. Often our values are in line with those of the company we work for, whether we've consciously evaluated that fit or arrived at it unconsciously. For example, at the time of writing, Google lists its 10 values online, a few of which are: focus on the user; do one thing really, really well; and fast is better than slow.

Values are a big part of who you are. Living your values makes you come alive; it's often when you feel 'in flow' in your life, when you're most satisfied. To determine your values, as a coach I would look for moments when you are exhibiting resonance about your life, when you are feeling the excitement, aliveness, vibration, and sheer energy associated with being alive. I invite you to notice when you feel this resonance as you complete the next exercise.

An Exercise to Enable You to Discover Your Values

Answer the following questions.[2] You don't have to answer them all, unless you want to. The key is in the description, the 'why' rather than the 'what' – the answer itself. I'll illustrate with two client examples. One client said they loved fondue because a fondue involves sharing with others, is social, slow, as it takes time, and consists of simple ingredients, and it is a ritual, rather than the mere fact they like melted cheese. Conversely another client liked Thai food because of its variety, spice, exotic origins, and because he only has it on special occasions. The contrast of these two descriptions points to very different values between these two clients.

Notice the patterns or themes that emerge across the various questions. Look for words and ideas that are repeated. Notice how you do the actual exercise. This in itself may point you to a personal value. Are you slow and methodical? Fast and laser-like? Do you hate picking just one favourite book or movie? If you like variety, then maybe there's something in this, the idea of choices, possibilities or options; of being free and unrestricted.

1. Describe a peak experience or a moment in time that was especially rewarding or poignant. Think of a particular moment such as walking across the stage to get your Certificate of Graduation from your university rather than the broad university experience.

2. What is your favourite food? Favourite meal? What is it about that food that you love?

3. What is your favourite movie? Favourite book? Again, what is it about that book? That movie?

4. Whom do you admire – dead, alive, real, fictitious, that you've known or never met? Why?

5. Describe a great day. It doesn't have to be a realistic narrative. Give your imagination free rein.

6. What do you despise? The opposite is probably a value.

7. What is your dream?

8. What was your childhood dream?

9. What must you have in your life? And why?

10. What inspires you?

11. Think of a recent important decision you made – what values were involved? What were you contributing?

12. Look at times when you overcame fear. What helped you?

13. When you are out in the daily world, what makes you smile?

14. What makes you jealous? It's probably something that you want for yourself.

The key to this exercise is to reflect on the answer and, once you've given it, look for the underlying factor that's important. Feel 'when the energy is resonant', which will mean it's important. Look for the common elements in your answers to these questions. What are the patterns or repetitive themes that arise? Circumstances do not equal values. In other words, 'family' is a circumstance. What is it about family that matters to you? What about 'family' brings you alive and energetic? It might be love, connection, legacy, community, safety or something else.

Of note, values can have a dark side. 'Love' is wonderful in terms of warmth, care and connection. If you love someone too much it can dominate your life, create unhealthy dependence and even suffocate you or the person whom you love.

Once you've started identifying the themes, patterns and repeating words, then group similar words or themes together to create value strings, since one word is not enough to communicate the full idea or essence. For example:

Integrity/honesty/walk the talk	vs	Integrity/whole/ congruent
Leadership/ collaborative/empower	vs	Leadership/decisive/ powerful

You can download my values exercise from my website at www.directions-coaching.com/

How Do Values Manifest Themselves at Work and in Your Life?

A sense of strong emotions is an indicator that values are present. It doesn't matter whether it's a positive/ light emotion or a negative/dark emotion. Of note, no emotion is really positive or negative, these are just labels by which we judge them. Your emotional response is the signal that a value you hold is being honoured or dishonoured. If you are frustrated or angry, the chances are that a value, something that is dear to you, is being dishonoured or stepped on. If you feel joy or fulfilment, the chances are that a value is being honoured.

You can find out other people's values by asking them some of the questions in the previous exercise. People telegraph their values with how they behave. For example, I generally walk extremely quickly, rarely because I'm late, more because I am determined and have a value around efficiency, so why dawdle? One caveat – make sure you seek supporting evidence of someone's values, if you don't want to stereotype them and make a fool of yourself. Some people walk fast because they are in a hurry!

Hopefully by now you at least have a rudimentary sketch of you as an individual with all your uniquenesses and complexities. What you capture here will be expanded on and used in the next Principle on self-awareness and self-management.

THE CHALLENGE

The purpose of this challenge is to know yourself better; to be more conscious of your motivations, preferences, and behaviours; to make your unconscious habits or default reactions more conscious.

Spend one hour this week pulling together all the data you have about you: performance reviews, assessments, feedback, stop/start/continue – and list your strengths, weaknesses, unique qualities and preferences. You can use the Johari Window framework if that helps you.

Spend another hour completing the values exercise as described above. What are the themes or patterns that emerge for you? Turn them into 4–7 value strings/ descriptions that capture what is important to you (remember, 'done is better than perfect').

Using these as a starting point, write down a minimum of 10 learnings or insights about yourself. Focus on the positives or observational commentary rather than making value judgements (good or bad).

BONUS TASK: Write your PPIN (Personal and Professional Identity Narrative) for a few hours this month – make it enjoyable. Perhaps this is an exercise you might complete down at the pub, or café, or in the garden or a place you enjoy.

Reflect on the exercise and the emerging themes:

▶ What did you learn about yourself?

▶ What did you notice about others? Often when our self-awareness increases, we start noticing things in other people too; differences as well as similarities.

▶ What habits, behaviours or values have helped you in life? Which have been less effective?

▶ What do you need to still learn or want to learn about yourself?

▶ What impact has your increased awareness had on how you behave and/or your state of being? On how you are going through your day?

▶ What did you notice on the first day of this challenge versus the fifth, in terms of your ability/comfort with knowing yourself?

You Think You Know Yourself? Go Deeper With More Self-Awareness, Self-Management And Conscious Choice

Develop More Self-Awareness

The challenges at the end of each Principle in this book are designed to increase your knowledge about yourself, bringing aspects of yourself more prominently into your consciousness. Self-awareness is often the first aspect of EQ because without knowing yourself it's difficult to know others and therefore even harder to navigate between you and them. The first step is to notice how you respond or react to the various stimuli you encounter.

The areas outlined below of physical, emotional and intellectual observations are not an exhaustive list. They describe three main areas of stimuli and sources of learnings, rather than anything more exhaustive. This book is a practical guide for people skills and hence the focus is on the major areas rather than subtler points you might get from a full-blown emotional intelligence book.

Physical: Notice Bodily Sensations

The easiest way to notice your reactions is to tune into the feelings or sensations in your body. This seems illogical in a work context. You might wonder, what does your body have to do with work and soft skills? Actually, the physical sensations in your body are data points that you can then analyze. For example, knots in your stomach can be an early warning alert for a bad situation. Tension in your neck can indicate stress before you are conscious of it. Each person has their own physical sensations that indicate fear, confidence, happiness, anxiety or sadness. Knowing how your body feels, noticing the physical sensations you are experiencing, often gives a heads-up that something is wrong or uncomfortable or positive. Remember in the Introduction to this book I mentioned the idea that nerves from our bodies go into our brain at the back through the brain stem and hence stimulate us before we've had the thought of what those sensations could mean.

The process of working on the challenges in this book will assist you in increasing your self-awareness as you go through your day. The practice of self-awareness itself creates greater awareness.

Emotional: Notice Emotions

Notice your emotions or feelings. What are your emotional reactions to people, situations, information, and even to your own thoughts? What brings you joy?

When do you feel love? What are you afraid of? What do you feel guilt or shame about and what makes you angry or causes pain? Your emotions are just another data set to teach you about yourself.

When I ask new clients how they are feeling, I often get responses such as 'fine', 'OK', or 'good'. These are not emotions and are often little more than socially acceptable responses before moving on to the 'real' topic of conversation such as what work needs to be done. Pia Mellody of The Meadow Treatment Centre theorizes that there are eight basic emotions: anger, fear, pain, joy, passion, love, shame and guilt.[1] Other emotional experts concur that there are a finite number of fundamental human emotions. I find the simplicity of so few emotions helpful for novices as it simplifies the choice and it's helpful for experts to get to the root feeling. Sometimes the nuances of language can mask, deny or diffuse an emotion to the point of rendering it unrecognizable. At other times the nuances of language can provide greater specificity.

For example: saying "I was angry" and feeling the strength of that emotion when I discovered the estate agent had not put forward my initial offer on the apartment I wanted to buy would have been more honest and real than saying "I was irritated or disgruntled." I was angry as it put me in a difficult situation when the developer replied to my subsequent offer by saying, "Let's split the difference." Since they hadn't seen my initial offer they didn't realize I had already moved significantly. Another example: "I feel content" is very different from saying "I feel joyful." The energy associated with each of these words is different to me.

Managing emotion is an area that didn't come naturally to me. When I was younger I was hardly aware of my emotions. I grew up in a quiet, rational, non-emotional family for the most part. I was an introverted, studious, fearful child. This continued through much of my early adult life. I even picked a life partner who had been raised similarly, where you don't delve into your emotions and everything appears calm on the surface. My emotions were there when I look back; I was just fearful of them so I repressed them or was in fact unconscious to them and lacked the vocabulary to label them or the environment in which to discuss them. Fear is an emotion and one that I was living with most of my early life. I identified that I lived in fear when I was in my thirties and then tried to avoid feeling it. I still didn't have the language to articulate it and I knew it was there. It wasn't until my parents' deaths (more about that in the last Part of this book, BEYOND) that I delved into the realm of emotions. Their deaths, within months of each other, broke me open. Now I know that feelings or emotions are often strong guiding forces when I am making decisions or assessing my experience in life. When I go on a date I notice how I feel when I am around the man. Do I feel confident, smart and adventurous, or cautious and scared, or bored and indifferent? How I feel when I'm with someone or in a particular situation is a great source of insight into how I view the world.

Psychologists say there are no such things as positive or negative emotions. Every emotion is what it is, and it is we who endow it with meaning. Let's be honest, there are some emotions we typically crave, such as

joy, love and passion, and others we shun, such as hurt,
shame and guilt. Every emotion has a light side and a
dark side. Carl Jung calls the dark side an emotion's
'shadow'. Try not to judge your emotions, simply start
by noticing them and then perhaps noticing what
meaning you attribute to them.

The Light Side and Dark Side of Emotions

Emotion	Light Side	Dark Side
Anger	Energy, heat, motivation	Hatred, aggression
Fear	Protection, warning	Restriction, powerless
Pain	Prevention, enlightening	Crippling
Joy	Energizing	Frivolous
Passion	Fuelling	Consuming
Love	Accepting	Blinding, dependent
Shame	Sensitivity	Cowering
Guilt	Reflection	Heavy

You may be asking yourself why feelings matter,
especially at work. Some clients have asked me that.
It's because your feelings are very much the experience
of your life. And the same is true for your staff. Think
of the good and bad times in your life. Your memory
contains both how you felt and the impact it had
on you. Also, there is a school of thought, led most
notably by Louise Hay in the 1970s, that emotions

have a direct correlation with health; both physical and emotional health. There are two powerful expressions that may be controversial, and which carry some undeniable truth:

1. **Disease in the body is dis-ease with something in life.**

   Some holistic practitioners believe that the physical ailments we experience as humans can be caused by incongruences in our thoughts and/or emotional state. Louise Hay in her book *You Can Heal Your Life* says, "we create every so-called illness in our body".[2] I don't believe that all physical ailments are caused by emotional blockages. I do believe that both my parents chose to die for emotional reasons. My father had lost his wife of 48 years in every way except physically to early stages of Alzheimer's and he was sad, angry and grieving for the loss of who she was and the partnership they shared. My mother was scared, confused and lonely after my father's death about who would take care of her as she knew she was incapable of being on her own.

2. **What you resist persists.**

   This is the modern contraction from psychologist Carl Jung's assertion. If you resist or deny feelings of hurt, sadness, and anger, those emotions will persist until you feel them, look at them, and acknowledge them and the situation that led to them.[3]

Intellectual: Notice Your Thoughts

Our mind generates thoughts, that's its job. It constantly assesses the environment and makes meaning of it. Sometimes we are conscious of this meaning and often we are not. When we flick a light switch on we rarely think of the electricity being generated at the electrical plant and then being transmitted through wires to the circuit board in our homes and from there to the physical switch opening the connection through the two terminals thus generating light from the bulb. If we thought of that detail for every mundane occurrence we'd have no time for anything else. Our unconscious mind provides us with practical shortcuts, so we accept how electricity works.

Where there are gaps in our information, our minds fill them in for us to make meaning. Often those meanings are **assumptions** as you don't always have all the information. Our minds make up stories all the time to create meaning and understanding in our lives. Let's take an example: at the local pub on Saturday night there was a man dressed in a felt fedora, a thick cream-coloured woollen scarf, and a black wool overcoat with a wool blazer underneath. He stood to the side of the dance floor listening to the band. He drank his pint of beer and tapped the glass with his finger. A couple of times he left his beer on the table, went out and smoked a cigarette and returned to the same spot, making others move away from the table despite it being crowded. Automatically my friend and I wondered what his story was. Is he an agent checking out the band, is he an owner of the pub evaluating the entertainment, and how come he's not sweating in a warm dance space? This reflection happened from just seconds of observation.

Thomas's Case Study Example – Self-Awareness

A senior leader, let's call him Thomas, who was promoted to the executive committee, was offered 1:1 executive coaching as part of a leadership program for all the executives. His objective for the coaching was to increase confidence, while his company's objective was to improve his strategic thinking. In our initial session he said he found it difficult to accept that he belonged on the executive committee, in large part because he was now a peer to leaders he had looked up to for a long time. As homework, I asked him to "notice how you feel in the exco meetings. Scan your body and remember the sensations. Notice the thoughts that go through your mind." He did and in our next session he was able to describe what was going on for him at those meetings, leading to his conclusion that he was often nervous and defensive, which meant he over-reacted when colleagues raised a question about his area of responsibility. Separately, his boss also gave him feedback that he was tense and stiff when meeting with the CEO. Thanks to the earlier homework he was able to identify what he was feeling and that he was trying to be perceived as professional and on top of everything.

Another aspect of your thoughts to notice is the critical voice in your head, the judgemental voice that tells you that "you aren't good enough" or "who do you think you are?" This voice is often called the **saboteur** because it can sabotage your efforts, it can hold you back or make you doubt yourself excessively. It comes from your past, your conditioning at home, in school or previous work.

If you want to investigate its origins, therapy can help you do that. There are times when this saboteur voice is beneficial, when it protects you from failing, from looking stupid, risking or making a mistake. It tries to keep you safe. It's a defence mechanism. The problem with it is that when you start trying new things and moving outside your comfort zone, your internal voice may not realize you are intentionally trying something new. Hence, your critical voice is conflicting with your desire to grow. It wants to keep you safe and small, to keep you in your comfort zone, to maintain the status quo. Sometimes when I hear that voice asking, "who do you think you are?", perhaps when I'm writing a book, I remind myself that the critical voice is a sign I'm stretching myself, which allows me to keep the voice at bay. Here are some examples of saboteur phrases and possible positive reframes:

Saboteur Phrases and Reframes

Critical Voice	Positive Reframe
I'm not good enough	I'm stretching myself and learn new stuff all the time
I can't do that	Up to now I haven't been able to do that, and I can learn
I'm stupid	I'm smart as demonstrated by my achievements to date
I'm afraid	Fear means I'm pushing my boundaries which is a good thing
I don't have time	I choose how I spend my time
I screwed up	I learn from my mistakes, perfection is not the goal

'They' won't like it	I've assessed the impact and have strategies to bring people along with me
'They'll' see I don't know	If I don't know, others probably don't know. Better to learn now than have a bigger issue later

Clients have identified saboteurs that have been intensively self-destructive. A female manager had a saboteur voice of "women don't make good leaders". Not at all helpful as she was pursuing advancement in her organization. Another male leader had a critical voice of "only self-important, arrogant people want to be in the c-suite". Again, not helpful, especially given his company was investing in the coaching to help prepare him for his next promotion.

Tips for Self-Awareness

- Watch yourself while you are *DOING* something (chairing a meeting, disciplining your child, cooking dinner) – to notice your thoughts, behaviours and reactions. Notice the running commentary you have in your head about yourself. What are your dominant scripts?

- Notice the assumptions you make. About people, situations, interactions, expectations. The horrible cliché 'to assume makes an ass of u and me' often rings true.

- Listen to the voice inside. How do you talk to yourself? What voice encourages you (or discourages you and undermines your confidence)?

- Be present 'in the moment' so you can observe, rather than ruminating over the past or anticipating the future.

- Notice your triggers. People being rude triggers me to anger as I place great worth on respect and integrity. Going into hospitals triggered fear as I previously associated hospitals with people being admitted and never leaving.

- Sit quietly and scan your body from head to toe. Notice all the sensations, without judging them. Take time and notice each of them and just be with them, and in doing that they often change with the attention.

- Which comes first? The thought? The feeling? The physical sensation? I think maybe the physical sensation and I'm not sure it matters. Pay attention when you notice something.

Awareness of Physical, Emotional, Energetic and Intellectual

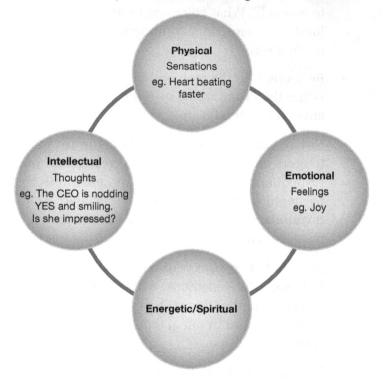

Create an Intentional Reputation – Personal and Organizational

When I ask leaders how they want their organization to be known in the industry, they often list: professional, successful, high quality and positive. The next type of question I ask, to go deeper, is "How would you differentiate your organization from your competitors around 'professional' for example?" The answers to that typically are: responsive to customers, organized, attentive and thorough. These answers start to get into the territory of soft skills, how people experience the organization.

I then ask about how they'd like to be known, themselves, as leaders; what reputation would they like to have in their organization and industry? Answers include: smart, approachable, helpful, knowledgeable, a good listener. Again, around the territory of soft skills, I ask how they interact with other people.

Questions in this space include:

> What first impression do you want to make?
>
> What lasting impression do you want to leave?
>
> How do you want to be known?
>
> How do you want your organization to be known?
>
> What reputation do you want in your industry?
>
> What reputation do you personally have and want within your organization?

Self-management doesn't mean changing who you are; it means being yourself with more skill, as urged by Rob Goffee and Gareth Jones in their book *Why Should Anyone Be Led By You?* Where are you effective? Where are you less effective? What abilities, qualities and talents can you lean into to be more effective? It's about improving your effectiveness to achieve your vision for yourself and the organization. That's why the first step is self-awareness, to know who you are.

Exercise More Skilful Self-Management

Self-management helps you to make the impression you want to make and have the impact you want to have. Self-management is the ability to respond rather than react. It's literally managing yourself, managing the time and space between what happens inside of yourself, based on some stimuli, and what you put out externally. Self-management happens between the physical sensations felt in your body/your emotions/ the thoughts in your head (which could have been stimulated by a third party) and your subsequent behaviours or actions. We are responsible for our reactions; we are **response-able** rather than at the mercy of our reptilian or limbic systems (fight, flight, or freeze). We can reflect on our emotions, sensations and thoughts and decide how to respond.

The importance of self-management is usually around negative thoughts, emotions and impulsive behaviour although it can happen around positive situations as well. It's required when our emotions have been triggered by something in a way that causes us to respond instinctively without determining the reality. For example, there had been errors in my electronic calendar for meetings entered by my PA (personal assistant), in one case even double-booking me without realizing it. This happened a few times. During our weekly phone call, we discussed it and it turned out that there was a syncing error between my laptop and phone, hence she couldn't see some of the diary entries I entered using my phone. Those phone entries didn't show up on the online calendar she viewed. We got my tech support guy on it. The next time I saw something that didn't make sense in my calendar I assumed she had made a mistake. Yes, I admit I assumed the worst even though we had an explanation. My default reaction was frustration with her until I changed my thought and reminded myself of the tech issue. And when I queried it, the tech issue had still not been solved fully.

A big component of being able to self-manage is to also manage your stress. People are more likely to react in unproductive ways or unconsciously when they are under too much stress. Some ideas for managing stress which you probably already know are:

- Have a healthy lifestyle (food, sleep, exercise, relaxation).

- Have a fulfilling hobby outside work.

- Take regular breaks in the work day.

- Connect and talk to people close to you including talking about how you feel.

- Have a reflective practice (journaling, meditation, mindfulness, spirituality, a moment of just saying 'calm' to yourself).

- Practise productive time management.

- Know your priorities and boundaries (say no).

- Have fun.

- Have a positive mental state as often as you can; when you notice your mental state is not positive, literally change the thoughts you're thinking to more positive ones.

The key to managing the stress is actually *living* most of these ideas, not just *knowing* them.

How to Self-Manage

1. Breathe – to be present and stay with whatever is coming up in your mind and body. Practise belly breathing. Put your hand on your stomach and breathe into your hand noticing your belly

rising and falling with each breath. You aren't actually breathing into your stomach, you're breathing into the full extent of your lungs. Very often, especially when stressed, we only breathe into the top part of our lungs. This deep breathing causes the relaxation response to kick in by triggering the activation of the parasympathetic system.[4] This is akin to the old adage that when you are angry, count to ten before responding. It's like hitting the 'pause button' on yourself.

2. Notice your patterns and responses over time. Either reflect on historical events or start noticing from now on, or both.

3. Name your thoughts and emotions. Label them. "Oh, I'm frustrated" or "I'm angry" or "I'm joyful" or "There's my desire to want her to stop crying" or "There's my reoccurring thought of being impatient with slow people". Stating the thought or what you are feeling makes them mere concepts to observe and be with, rather than empirical truths that need to be resolved or acted upon. By making them tangible they stay as distinct snippets and not unyielding ramblings. Often if you name something it lessens its emotional power over you.

4. Determine which serve you and which don't. Examine your most frequent reactive responses and patterns to see if they achieve the outcome you want. Reflect back on occasions when you exhibited each reaction.

What was the outcome? What was the impact on the other person? How did you feel during it and afterwards? Were you honouring your values or not? Were you creating the reputation you want? The answers to these questions will help you decide if those reactions serve you or not.

5. For those that serve you (get you the result you want, make you feel good about yourself, make others feel good in the process), keep doing what you are doing. And celebrate your success in who you are being during the interaction. Be proud (not arrogant or boastful). Practise being with your positive attributes and accomplishments – doing so allows you to be with others' good qualities and role-models for them how to be with their positives.

6. For those that don't serve you – because they aren't aligned to your values, don't move you towards your goals, don't aid the organization in achieving its goals or make others feel good – brainstorm some alternative stories that would result in a better feeling and outcome. Literally, ask yourself: What might be causing this situation? What are some other perspectives for the other person? What are some other possibilities of my role in this? How might the other person see it? How might an external, third party see it? What different responses or actions are possible from each of these new stories?

Lydia's Case Study Example – Self-Management

A client, we'll call her Lydia, noticed she was frustrated and disappointed with one of her staff. She realized that she felt impatient with him *(labelling thoughts and feelings)*. When she reflected on why, it was because he always asked her what to do. For homework between sessions I asked some questions to ponder the possible stories of what might be going on: "What might be causing him to do this?" Her initial 'stories' were: he's lazy, he can't think for himself. "What are some other stories?" She offered up: maybe he's not qualified for the job, maybe he's worried about making a mistake, maybe he's stressed and overworked. "What could be some stories of your role in this dynamic?" She admitted this was the hardest question, which took her some time to answer. The possibilities were: he didn't know what was expected of him, I have a certain way I want things done, he's worried I'll be disappointed with how he decides to do it, I tell him what to do a lot of the time. When she brought these reflections to our next session it was as simple as asking "Which story or stories serve you best?" and "What possible actions would you want to try from this perspective?" The initial feeling of disappointment/shame she had in herself for blaming him for everything when she probably had contributed to it, if not caused it, was quickly replaced with motivation to try something different and hope for something better.

7. Practise your alternative action next time you're in that familiar pattern. If you know your response isn't ideal with a particular individual, prepare in advance. Set an intention of the ideal response you want to have prior to meeting that person. Be accountable to yourself for your growth and transformation.

8. Reflect afterwards what worked and what didn't with that alternative action.

9. Repeat. This takes practice hence the need to repeat.

Getting Comfortable with the Discomfort

Self-management takes practice. Just as it took time for you to learn how to ride a bicycle or drive a car, it takes time to learn self-management. It will be awkward and uncomfortable at first. You might feel pulled in many directions as you're focusing on the work at hand, the interaction with the other person, observing yourself and all the thoughts in your head including the reminder to scan your body. The discomfort arises because you start noticing your responses and try to stop your reaction if it's not productive or helpful, and then try to quickly figure out what is a more effective response. You might feel like you are stumbling, as if tripping over yourself rather than smoothly, effortlessly being in an interaction. It can feel like that because that is what is happening; you react, then realize you reacted and then try to reverse the action, and then try to make a more productive response and then wonder if that was in fact better, repeat! Be kind to yourself. You are moving from an instinctive reaction to a conscious response.

Thomas's Case Study Example Continued – Self-Management

Once Thomas was aware of his lack of confidence, being defensive and appearing stiff (from his own reflections and from direct feedback from his boss), we worked on (i) how he wanted to feel and (ii) how he wanted to be perceived.

The first step was for him to identify what he wanted. He wanted to feel like an equal at the executive table, like a partner in the business with the other executives. He wanted to feel relaxed, comfortable and enjoy the experience with his colleagues and the CEO. We explored times in his life (personally and professionally) when he felt relaxed, confident, comfortable and most like himself. He recreated those feelings within himself so he knew what confident and relaxed felt like in his body. He named the feeling Tom (in contrast to him being called Thomas at work), and used the label 'rugby' to describe how he wanted to be part of the team, and the visual of a light switch to help him pause and relax.

From those descriptions, we designed some structures to remind him during the meetings of how he wanted to be and feel and how he wanted to show up. He had a picture of himself from his rugby days on a mug he took into the meeting, a drawing of a light switch on a small sticky note on his papers, and the name Tom on the front of his notebook. These structures would help him remember what he wanted to practise when/if he went 'unconscious' during the meetings.

As Thomas's case illustrates, another way of being with the discomfort is to have visual reminders or structures to support you with the new behaviours and mindset you're experimenting with. This idea has similarities to Neuro-Linguistic Programming anchoring – the process of associating an internal feeling to an external stimulus. The stimulus triggers the feeling within you and can be accessed when needed. Helpful structures should be:

- Things that you can easily see so when you're pressured or busy you don't have to go looking for the reminder.

- Obvious to you and unrecognizable in their purpose to others.

- Things that evoke the behaviour and ideally the positive feeling associated with that experiment.

- Changed when it becomes wallpaper, no longer reminding you of your goal.

- Fun, light, playful.

- Examples are sticky notes, words written at the top of a page, a photograph, a drawing by your child, a mug or pen (as these are common in workplaces), a ring or bracelet (as you see it when you're talking), or any other ideas.

Another way of being with the discomfort is staying present, living in the present moment. There are three timeframes from which to live: the past, the present and the future. All are worthwhile when appropriate. The past is worthy of reflection to learn and grow (therapy, lessons learned from a completed project). The future is worthy when visioning (for work or life). The present is worthy most of the rest of the time. When you feel discomfort it's often because you're comparing it to a feeling in the past or worried about some impact in the future. The discomfort in the moment is often not so big when you're just with it, with no comparison or what if. Ways of staying present, two of which I've already mentioned, are:

1. Breathing into your belly

2. Feeling the physical sensations such as feeling your feet firmly on the floor

3. Using the word 'now'

4. Slowing down – your breath, your mind, your speaking, your movements

5. Focusing on what's in front of you, the task at hand, the other person (to avoid multi-tasking and going inside yourself)

Step into Fully Conscious Choice

This is an extension of self-management and so important I wanted to make it very distinct.

Conscious choice is about choosing consciously. It's about choosing your response, your decision, your behaviour with full awareness that it's your choice. So often I and others do things out of habit or unconsciousness. I was out to dinner with two friends last week and one suggested they buy a bottle of wine rather than two glasses as the cost of the third glass, if either of them were to have it, would be more than the bottle. The second friend replied "sure". It was only the next day, reflecting on having drunk half a bottle of wine, that she realized she just went along with the other's suggestion rather than what she wanted. She said if she had stopped and thought about it she would have realized she only wanted one glass and would have stuck to that decision rather than being so easily swayed. Conscious choice isn't about limiting yourself; if she had consciously chosen to share the bottle, that would have been a good decision too; it's about the consciousness rather than the amount of alcohol in this example.

Choices = Possibilities Not Limitations

Conscious choice is about recognizing all the options you often have in front of you. Not the sheer quantity rather the possibilities within any given situation. This is best illustrated when in debate with another person and each of you has your own idea of the best solution to a problem. You think solution A is best, your colleague feels solution B is best. Do you negotiate between those two solutions, highlighting all the rational reasons why yours is best? And they do the same with their idea? What about all the possibilities between the two? Maybe a third solution is actually the best one? And there are probably many more than three available to choose from.

I was part of a trio tasked with putting on an act or skit of some sort for a talent show amongst a group of close colleagues – no limits to what we could do, use, or depict. The other woman in my trio wanted to depict her Scandinavian roots by being bundled up in layers of clothes on a snowy mountain. The man in our trio said he wanted to end up naked at the end of our skit. Talk about polar opposites! I had no idea as I don't act, hate talent shows and I'm dire at frivolity. After the initial brainstorming we were at an impasse, no idea what to do, no idea how bundled on a mountain and naked could co-exist, and our planning time was over for now. At the end of our afternoon session I had a brainwave of how these two things could co-exist and be profound (which is what I wanted)! We did a skit about our personal development journeys: starting off wrapped up, insulated on treacherous peaks and in dark valleys, and ending in our underwear, showing the layers having been stripped away and our vulnerability there for all to see. Our resulting skit was a co-creation of two polar opposites with full choice amongst the three of us to be next-to-nude in front of our colleagues. We were committed.

Thomas's Case Study Example Continued – Conscious Choice

With the visual reminders at hand of how he wanted to feel and be, Thomas practised invoking the feeling of confidence when it was waning in the meetings. He risked injecting humour and personality into a presentation as that's what Tom would do.

He noticed when he became defensive on receiving an email from a colleague challenging a decision. He felt undervalued, frustrated and angry. He half-wrote a reply, deleted it and in the end decided to have a face-to-face to discuss it so he could 'practise' asking questions. Getting curious about what prompted the email from his colleague in the first place allowed him to find out what was going on for that colleague and not make assumptions before addressing the actual decision being challenged.

Additionally, after a couple of meetings he asked his boss for feedback on how he was coming across. He felt "that meeting with the CEO was the best ever. It felt so relaxed and positive." His personality was evident, and he was enjoying the promotion more.

Conscious choice isn't just about deciding something and getting on with it. It is about realizing the power you have with every choice you make. There's a **freedom and responsibility** to choosing. At the extreme you have a choice in each moment, you can choose what you do or say at every instance and you are responsible for the choices you make. That responsibility means you are committing to something and often someone; there's no turning back. There's integrity about following through.

How You Make Choices

How you make choices also reveals things about yourself. Do you choose quickly or slowly and deliberately? Do you ponder options at length? Do lots of complex analysis? Spend the same amount of time and effort whatever the choice being made – your baby's name versus what to order at the coffee shop?

Choice is about **prioritizing**. We can't do everything we want all the time. Think about your priorities, both in work and life, or professionally and personally as I like to call it, as work is part of life. What are your priorities within each category? There's always a balance between the number of priorities that are motivating and possible versus burnout – easy to say, harder to do. Your values, your intuition, your physical sensations, how you want to feel and the reputation you want to build for yourself, are all factors in making these choices.

Potential Personal and Professional Priorities

Professional	Personal
Corporate Objectives	Family
Key Projects	Health
Growing Your People	Financial
Career Progression	Spiritual/Leisure
Social Responsibility	Home
Financials	Friends

Whenever there is a choice there is the option of saying YES or NO. Very simple words and when talking about conscious choice and commitment they are very profound. Whenever you say YES to something, you are saying NO to something else. When you say YES to working late, you are saying NO to joining your family for dinner. As an aside, some clients struggle with saying NO to a request or a new piece of work. I ask them: "By saying YES to that new demand, what would you be saying NO to?" Because those clients would be saying NO to something. They don't have hours of idle time to fill, they are busy, successful people with families and outside interests. Often, they would be saying NO to meeting the deadlines of their own projects, their family, their wellbeing, or their leadership development time. So rather than focusing on the NO and disappointing the person immediately in front of you, say YES to your conscious priorities. If you are only willing or able to say 'I guess I will' to something, say NO, at least until you can say 'Absolutely Yes!!' The enthusiasm and boldness of your YESes or NOs should tell you something about how wholeheartedly you are committing to it or not.

**The Cycle of Self-Awareness, Self-Management and
Conscious Choice**

This challenge is big as it's the end of the INSIDE Part of the book, so although it's not the last time you'll reflect on you, I want to encourage you to journal as much as possible before you turn your attention to the OUTSIDE.

THE CHALLENGE

Continue to become aware of yourself in every way possible.

▶ Do you go first when given a choice, or go last? For example, in a group situation where everyone is equal and someone says, "who wants to go first?", do you volunteer to jump in or hang back?

▶ What do you do when you're angry or frustrated?

▸ Do you speak without much forethought or ponder considerably before speaking?

▸ What's your reaction if criticized? Or if you realize you've made a mistake?

▸ What situations or people blind you?

▸ What impact is stress having on you with regard to self-management?

▸ When are you contemplative of your response and when are you reactive?

▸ What do the voices in your head say? What are their critical messages? What are their supportive messages?

When would it serve you to manage yourself better? By containing yourself, listening rather than speaking, being less explosive, sitting still? Or by letting yourself go, such as making yourself heard, being vulnerable, asking questions, showing acceptable emotion, being expressive?

What reputation do you want personally and for the organization?

With everything you have learned about yourself from the INSIDE Part of this book, what conscious choices are you making?

▸ Around leveraging your strengths?

▸ Interacting with someone in a different way?

▸ To stretch outside your comfort zone?

▸ To regulate an ineffective or unproductive reaction?

▸ To have more fun and enjoy your journey?

▶ What are you choosing to keep so that it's not blind habit?

▶ What reputation do you want to create, strengthen, leverage?

▶ What commitments are you wanting to make and willing to keep?

▶ How do you feel physically in various situations?

▶ What are you saying **YES** to?

Write down your choices in your journal, simple sentences, nothing convoluted. Prioritize the list. Focus on three things for today. You can come back to the other things on the list later.

Choice 1:

Choice 2:

Choice 3:

Stand up (close your office door or go into a conference room if you're worried about someone seeing you). Put a line down on the floor in front of you; it can be a line of masking tape, a string, a ridge in the carpet, the edging of a tile or, at a pinch, a pen. Stand on one side of this 'line' and say *"I consciously choose [insert one thing/action/intention you are choosing]"* and step across the line. Stepping over that line represents your commitment. Don't step across that line if you aren't ready to fully commit. This is the powerful choice exercise I do with my executive clients that creates even more commitment when witnessed by me (or someone else).

Now that you've chosen consciously – what are two actions you will take this week to move one of those three choices forward? Choice without action is really just hopes and dreams.

Choice 1, 2 or 3:

Action 1 –

Action 2 –

Reflect on the exercise and topic:

- ▶ What did you learn about yourself and about self-management?

- ▶ What did you learn about yourself around choosing and committing?

- ▶ What do you need to still learn?

- ▶ What impact did it have on how you are behaving?

- ▶ What did you notice the first day versus the fifth in terms of your commitments to yourself?

PART 2

OUTSIDE

We will pause the self-reflection and fast-forward to looking outside yourself. For some it's a relief not to be focused on themselves, it feels too indulgent or selfish or unproductive. For some it feels good to spend time in the reflective space because you like it or because it's something new to you. For the former, sorry to say we will return to you. For the latter, don't worry, we'll come back to YOU shortly in Part 3.

This OUTSIDE section is about putting the focus on the other person; it's not about you. For some of you this will feel very natural, the area where you spend most of your time; on other people individually or in a group or team. For others it might be foreign territory where people are just a means to an end, a vehicle to deliver what is needed. The spin on this OUTSIDE perspective is for you to put your attention on another person, in service of them and their needs. Notice where I am directing you to place your attention now – outside of yourself towards another individual for their benefit. Not for your gain, rather for their gain. In the purist state of focusing on others or being in service of others you would suspend your goals or agenda. There is an implicit belief in this idea of letting go of your agenda and helping others – that if you care about their needs and wants you will ultimately achieve your agenda, it just might be in a different way than you expect.

Part 2 will cover the three Principles of feedback, coaching and storytelling. These are three tools and ways of interacting with others that help them increase their effectiveness.

The feedback section will cover both positive and negative (or constructive) feedback; yes, feedback can be positive too! It itemizes the benefits of giving feedback, the aversions of why people don't do it, and illustrates a model of what to do and how to do it. It's a true list of advice and ideas with plenty of examples to help you formulate your own feedback.

The coaching section will differentiate between *coaching* and *telling* when interacting with employees (or anyone else). It will highlight the benefits of each mode of communication, tips for doing it well, with a model of what to do and how.

The storytelling section covers the fears and benefits of storytelling and again shows what to do and how to do it.

This Part is very practical with models, tips, tricks and examples. It's written to appeal to your structured and analytical approach. There are lots of things for you to try, do and practise from this section – so you can imagine the challenge at the end of each Principle already!

Actively Give (And Solicit) Feedback

Giving feedback is a great place to start the OUTSIDE section. It is about putting your attention on another person – a team member, employee, peer or even boss – noticing the other person's behaviours, qualities and/or results. And then actually communicating those specific observations to that individual for their growth, and let's not get ahead of ourselves.

When I say feedback to my leadership training participants and executive clients there's usually a noticeable cringe, signifying discomfort, and often the response is "I'm not good at those difficult conversations." Amazing how feedback is associated with discomfort and difficulty. It's almost always assumed to be negative, a 'big' conversation, and telling someone something that they are doing wrong.

As an aside, *having reached Principle 3 you are open and committed to learning or new ideas – keep reading through to Principle 10.* That sentence you just read was actually feedback! It wasn't negative or constructive, it wasn't difficult, and it didn't point out anything you were doing wrong. It was just an observation served up in a skilful way. What impact did it have on you?

In this section you'll learn the reasons stopping you from giving both negative and positive feedback.

Like many of the practices in this book, the secret of success is plenty of practice. I want to encourage you to normalize feedback, so that it simply becomes the way you manage, rather than a tough chore to be endured. An important concept about where to give and receive feedback will be shared in a bullseye visual to equip you to think on your feet in the moment when feedback is so powerful. And lastly a feedback model will provide you with structure for giving both positive and negative feedback. The skill comes in how you use the model, which will be illustrated through a list of tips and many examples.

Giving Feedback

First, let's start with what stops most people from giving feedback.

Top Reasons People Don't Give Negative/ Constructive Feedback

1. It will demotivate them and I need them motivated

2. I don't want to hurt their feelings

3. I don't know how to do it so I don't. What if I get it wrong?

4. I want people to like me

5. I don't have time to do it

6. They should know better already

7. I've got too many other things to do

8. I meant to, just didn't get around to it

9. I figured it out for myself, they need to figure it out on their own

10. I don't know why they don't get it, what could I say to change it?

Top Reasons People Don't Give Positive Feedback

1. I'd have to give them a raise and there's no money in the budget

2. I'd have to promote them and there's no spots available

3. They should do well, it's their job, they are getting paid to do it

4. It will go to their heads, we don't need more divas working here

5. No one ever praised me!

6. I'm British, we don't do that

7. They know they've done well

8. I don't know how to do it

9. What if I get it wrong?

10. I said 'great job' and 'thanks', isn't that enough?

Benefits of Giving Feedback

The benefits of giving feedback are almost too obvious to state – and they are the same whether the feedback is positive or negative/constructive.

1. Your team feel valued because overall you give noticeably more positive feedback than negative/constructive (research says financially successful companies give positive feedback 5–6 times for every one piece of negative feedback given).[1] People feel that you care about their performance and hence about them because you are taking time to communicate specifics with them.

2. Your co-workers learn what you expect and what success looks like because you reinforce it when you point out the positives and illustrate what better looks like when you point out an improvement.

3. You are seeing and hearing your colleagues as individuals and they will respect you for that.

4. You create a feedback culture in the organization thereby encouraging everyone to contribute to good/better performance.

5. Colleagues learn to improve ineffective actions or feel you reinforce their existing positive behaviour thereby positively impacting the business.

6. Company performance improves (see research referenced in #1 above).

7. You are perceived as observant, engaged and a people-person (by your team and potentially peers and superiors).

8. Expressing concerns (and requests) openly and honestly when they arise prevents bottling up of resentment and frustration which, if unsaid, could lead to illness, an explosive tirade or damaged relationships.

Where to Give (and Receive) Feedback

One of the keys to giving effective feedback is to direct the feedback towards something the person can change or improve (or continue if it's positive). Someone can change their behaviours and skills. It's much more difficult for someone to change an aspect of their personality or identity, and hearing negative feedback about your personality or character is usually painful.

The Logical Levels, used as a tool or model in Neuro Linguistic Programming (NLP) and developed by coach, consultant and trainer Robert Dilts and Todd Epstein, is a useful structure to assess where to give and receive feedback. The levels are illustrated overleaf.

Where to Give and Receive Feedback[2]

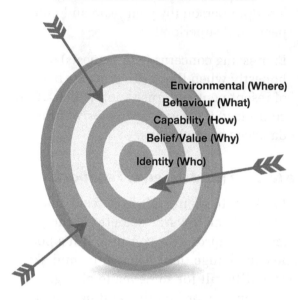

Environmental (Where)
Behaviour (What)
Capability (How)
Belief/Value (Why)
Identity (Who)

Give feedback primarily at the outer level of the bullseye rather than the centre. Give (and receive) feedback at a behaviour or capability level as these are areas within a person's control. Feedback at an environment level is suitable too, although the person might be limited in how they can effect change. Refrain from giving feedback at the level of someone's identity, beliefs or values as this is fundamental to the person and really not up for change. The same approach holds true when you are receiving feedback. If someone is giving you feedback, get clarity from them at a behaviour or ability level, don't take feedback at an identity level – you are worthy as a human being regardless of their comments. The following illustrates the levels from the outward position of someone's environment to an inward position at the core or centre of who they are as a person.

Example: Imagine a manager giving a presentation about a new initiative to the Board. The projector light bulb blows part way through, so they are unable to use the overhead to show their PowerPoint slides. Nevertheless, the Board still approve the initiative to proceed. I'll illustrate feedback at each level using a classic two-point style of feedback: "When you... then..."

Environment level – this refers to the physical situation, the WHERE, the space in which the person was working.

> Feedback example: "When the projection of the presentation stopped, it was great that you had handouts of key slides to share so the Board could still follow along."

OR

> "It would have been more impactful and memorable to do the presentation in the laboratory where the initiative will take place rather than in a meeting room."

Behaviour level – this refers to the specific behaviours the person is doing or words they are saying, the WHAT.

> Feedback example: "When you remained calm and listened intently while the Director was aggressively questioning your rationale you earned respect from others in the room and were able to answer his concerns in a succinct and convincing manner thereby persuading him."

OR

> "When you interrupted Tom in the meeting the effect was that you appeared defensive."

Capability level – this refers to the level of someone's ability to perform a task or skill; it's the HOW. Often this level relates to the competency they've shown from training they've had, or the need for training to build their ability.

> Feedback example: "You presented both emotional and rational arguments in support of your recommendation, I can see you leveraged those elements from that influencing course you took."

OR

> "I recommend you take a presentation skills course to learn and practise how to present without PowerPoint slides."

Beliefs/Values level – this is the level of someone's values or beliefs, WHY they do or feel as they do. It's best to avoid feedback at a values level. Occasionally it's OK at a beliefs level if the belief is a limiting belief that is not serving the individual (such as a belief they are not good at presenting when they are good). Remember in Principle 2 you identified your saboteur and some of the critical voices in your head? This is the same for others, so if you notice a limiting belief or critical script, you can ask about that, just don't negate their healthy values or beliefs.

> Feedback example: "You showed integrity not acquiescing to the demand to change the launch timing."

OR

> "You should have given into the argument challenging the timing of the initiative going live."

Identity level – this refers to the person at their identity level, WHO they are. It's best never to give feedback at this level; this is about the person as a human being. Particularly in the case of negative feedback this can be damaging to anyone's confidence and sense of self. There's nothing the person can really do with this type of feedback.

"You were brilliant." (while this might feel good and be well received it does little to give the individual tangible, specific details of what they can repeat for a future positive outcome)

OR

Feedback: "You were an idiot (stupid)."

Using a Feedback Model

The What

There is a simple four-step model that many people recommend, and I will follow suit. It's called the C.O.I.N. model and can be used for giving both positive and negative/constructive feedback. It's so simple, so please keep it simple, this is a great case of less words are more effective.

C is for context or circumstances, the when and where of the situation.

O is for what was observed, the action or behaviour exhibited.

I is for the impact it had, on you, the team, another individual, or the business.

N is for next steps, what you expect or encourage the recipient to do next with the feedback.

The COIN Feedback Model

	Description	Example of How to Communicate
C	What situation or circumstance has prompted this feedback? Where was the individual? When did it occur?	At the meeting this morning... Yesterday in the office... On the phone Monday...
O	What did you observe? What specific action or behaviour have you seen or heard at the given moment? What did the person do or say on which you want to give feedback?	When you did... When you said... When you didn't say/do... What I observed was... What I saw was... I noticed...
I	What impact did that action or behaviour have on you, potentially others, the business, or in the room? This can be tangible like someone walking out of a meeting, or intangible like a feeling.	The impact of that was... The effect of that was... The result was... It made me/others feel... It caused... I felt... The team felt...
N	What is the desired next step you would like the recipient to do with the feedback? What behaviour or action would you like them to do in the future?	Next time I suggest you... What I would want you to do is... My advice would be... In the future you could try... My preference would have been... I encourage you to...

The COIN Feedback Model In Action

	Example of Positive Feedback	Example of Constructive Feedback
C	In today's project review meeting...	When I was walking around the floor this afternoon...
O	I noticed when Marc expressed his concern over the launch timing you paused, nodded your head, asked a couple of open-ended questions and asked, "this sounds important to you, can we set up some separate time to discuss it?"	I saw you leaning over your sales manager advising him that he could have been more structured when answering the customer's questions in the customer meeting this morning.
I	When you listen to people, ask clarifying questions, acknowledge someone, even if junior to you – Marc feels more valued, the idea of raising concerns is encouraged thereby mitigating risks, and others in the meeting respect you even more.	The impact on him could have been embarrassment and intimidation. And because you are a manager, others in the open-plan office might have felt uncomfortable and that you were being disrespectful.
N	Well done. Keep up the good work. Thanks for role-modelling those skills to the attendees.	In the future please deliver constructive feedback eye-to-eye and ideally in your office. It's better to be on 'the same level' and to punish in private and praise in public.

You can download a template for a COIN discussion from my website at www.directions-coaching.com/

The How

The HOW is so important for the feedback to be perceived as genuine and constructive and for it to be received positively. You know what it feels like if someone gives you a beautifully wrapped, timely, perfect-for-your birthday present versus someone just tossing you a creased card a day late that they bought at the corner shop.

- Give the feedback as close to the action/behaviour observed as possible (so it's fresh in everyone's minds).

- Give feedback daily, don't wait for performance reviews or "extreme situations that require attention". Make it a daily practice.

- Give positive feedback in public if appropriate and the recipient likes that attention (or at least can tolerate the attention).

- Give negative/constructive feedback in private to avoid being perceived as critical or causing embarrassment or shame (there's a well-known expression to help you remember the last two tips: praise in public, punish in private).

- Speak slowly and clearly, being as specific as possible. Pause slightly after O (after you tell them what you observed), pause slightly after I (the impact it had), and then stop talking after N (stating the next step).

- Use the minimum number of words possible. More detracts from the clarity of the message.

- Check for comprehension, that they understand what you have said. Ask them "what clarification can I provide?" or "what would you like me to repeat to ensure I've been clear?" or "what's your understanding of what I said?"

- Look them in the eye (softly, not laser-like) and smile (just look pleasant, not a creepy smiley-face).

- Be patient with yourself and the recipient.

- Have the intention of being of service to that person, of giving them a gift, of wanting them to grow and develop (versus "given feedback tick √"), have it come from your heart rather than just your head.

- Remember, just as you are free to give feedback, so the person to whom you are giving it is free to listen (or not), adopt, adapt or reject what you have said. Don't assume and don't expect!

- If it is difficult feedback, give the person some time and space to digest it. Say "I sense you might need time to process/digest/think about what I said. Let's meet tomorrow to talk about it again" (and if you said to meet tomorrow, then you follow up with them and talk about it. This is not the time to get skittish. Don't expect the recipient to follow up proactively until you've created a feedback culture/reputation).

THE CHALLENGE

Give positive feedback using the model above every day for the next five days.

Practise at least five times per day with five different people using the full COIN model in a 1:1 conversation.

Try it in both your professional and personal life. For example, I just did this in the coffee shop where I am writing this section of my book. I told Alex, the server, "Your cheery welcoming of customers and pleasant eye contact makes me and I'm sure others feel welcome and wanted here, thank you."

After five days of giving positive feedback, practise giving small negative/constructive feedback (don't make stuff up, focus on something genuine). Do this at least once a week.

Reflect each time you do it:

▶ What did you learn about yourself when using the model? About others?

▶ What worked well? What do you need to still practise?

▶ What impact did it have? Either tangible (what people said to you about it) or intangible (what you feel/sense the impact was)?

▶ What are the differences between giving positive and negative feedback?

▶ What have you noticed about other people when they give feedback? What works? What doesn't?

▶ What's the best feedback you've received? What was good about it in terms of content and delivery?

▶ What did you notice the first day versus the fifth in terms of your ability/comfort?

PRINCIPLE 4

Choose A Coaching Approach More Often Than Telling

Coaching is close to my heart. It's a passion for me, not just a profession or set of skills or a model; it's often how I'm 'being' when I'm interacting in the world. When I dated a widower with 6-year-old twin boys, occasionally I had to parent. I didn't know how to parent, so I coached. Coaching or the skills that contribute to being a successful coach, which this section will cover, has application in many areas of human interaction. The elements shared here are some skills and techniques as they relate to the organizational needs of coaching; it doesn't delve into the psychology of human behaviour. I retrained as a coach after my 'mid-life crisis' when I was searching for more meaning in my life after the deaths of my parents. Oh, I'm getting ahead of myself.

With this Principle you'll learn the difference between coaching and telling – both are important skills at work and in life; the key is knowing when to use which, given the situation and people involved. I'll share the reasons to tell and the reasons to coach. I'll share a model for telling and a model for coaching. There will be more information on coaching than telling to be honest; most leaders know how to tell already, whereas many need more tools and encouragement to coach.

Telling

I included telling in this section as a contrast to coaching. Telling is a useful skill to have as a leader, telling people what to do and how to do it. You have years of experience, you've seen lots of issues and been in numerous complex situations. You have lots to share. There are many people in your organization who want your contribution to assist them with their responsibilities.

And sometimes telling is detrimental. It creates dependency, it's slower in the long run if you always have to tell, as you don't enable someone to think for themselves, and it limits diversity of ideas as it's always your thoughts you are perpetuating.

Top Reasons People Tell

- It's fast, certainly faster than teaching, coaching or training.

- It's so natural that it's unconscious; you don't even have to think about it.

- It's efficient as people go in the direction you want them to go in *(they do it right, your way)*.

- It's a critical situation, e.g. "Get out, the building is on fire!"

- "They just want to be told rather than figure it out on their own."

- "They are new/inexperienced and just don't know."

- "I've got the answers, why make people struggle or guess?"

When It's Good to Tell

- When you're teaching someone a new skill or doing knowledge transfer

- When you're training someone in a specific activity

- When it's a crisis or critical

- If you've tried repeatedly to coach and encourage them and they haven't grasped it

The How of Telling (When Not a Crisis)

1. Plan what you want to tell them

   a. Put yourself in the other person's shoes to assess what they need or want

   b. Why you are telling them this, what's the context or the purpose behind it?

   c. Be specific with your communication – err on the side of more clarity than you think necessary

   d. Think about the time after you tell them what to do – what's required as follow up, if anything?

2. Tell them what you want to tell them

    a. Make it a discussion not a one-way lecture

    b. Check that they have understood

    c. Agree what happens next

3. Follow up

    a. If agreed, follow up as you said you would, when you said you would

    b. If no follow up is required, it may be an opportunity for you to give positive feedback, e.g. if you told them how to access a system and you notice they are doing it well, then tell them (see feedback section above)

Coaching

Coaching is a skill, a set of tools and also a mindset. What I'm presenting here is coaching as a skill and set of tools. This will not make you a certified coach; this will assist you in using coaching skills as an option in your toolbox of leadership skills.

Benefits of Coaching

- People learn to think their way through a situation, enabling them, making them less reliant on you.

- People bring their ideas and thoughts to the situation which might result in new, unique solutions and more creativity and diversity of thinking.

- It's less work for you in the long run as you train them to figure it out (make them more independent and empower them when it is done well).

- You don't have to know everything all the time (which might be a blow to your ego).

- People feel valued and heard and often are more engaged as they are genuinely asked to explore their ideas.

- You develop leaders, grow greater talent, thereby growing the organization's capability (and it just might be more fulfilling for you).

The What of Coaching

Coaching is really just the creation of a reflective space for someone (the client or coachee or employee) to figure out their own solutions and ideas in relation to a particular topic. This is done by the coach (or leader in your case) listening in a deep and non-judgemental way and asking open (sometimes powerful) questions that help the employee discover ideas and possibilities in themselves.

I've coached people for 10 minutes who were passing by on the street (it was part of a street team providing free coaching in London) and been given feedback that they found the experience profound. I've coached people for hours to the same result, meaning coaching can be 10 minutes, 30 minutes, an hour or longer – depending on the situation, topic, what they want out of it and the time you have.

1. Listening is the starting point for great communication including coaching. Through my coach training with the Co-Active Training Institute (CTI), I learned there were three levels to listening, which changed how I listen and engage (most of the time).[1]

The Three Levels of Listening

Level 1 – Internal Listening/ Focused on self	Your focus is on yourself, your thoughts, feelings, issues. When someone mentions a topic you immediately go to your thoughts, feelings and opinions on that topic. It's about your internal narrative or conversation.
Level 2 – Focused Listening on the other	Your focus is on what the other person is saying in a laser-like fashion, as though you're under the 'cone of silence' in the old *Get Smart* TV program. When someone mentions a topic, you want to know that person's thoughts, feelings and opinions about the topic. You have little awareness of the outside world.
Level 3 – Focused on the whole or Global Listening	Your focus is on everything, the space, what's going on inside you and with the other person, what's going on energetically. This is where intuition or gut-feel might come in; the action, inaction and interaction.

2. Questioning is the second important factor to good coaching; it's about being curious, so the employee gets curious. Formulate your questions based on what the employee says; use their actual words to formulate questions that help them delve deeper to greater understanding. Use open questions (which can't be answered with 'yes' and 'no'). Keep the questions short (as this focuses the thinking and doesn't confuse things). Ask "so what?" after almost any question to get the employee to keep thinking or go deeper.

3. The GROW model, first published by John Whitmore in his book *Coaching for Performance* in 1992, is a widespread framework to use when coaching.[2] It might not seem sophisticated being just four simple steps and yet it can be incredibly powerful. When clients have practised this in group coaching they are often struck by how often they just want to tell the person the/their answer; how they have so many ideas going through their own head they find it hard paying attention to what the other person is saying; how often they ask closed and leading questions; and how they want to speed up the process, even if the person is not ready. Some have been amazed at how often the coachee generated tremendous value from the exercise even if the coach had no idea what was being talked about! Remember coaching is about the other person solving the problem or generating the solution, not your understanding as the coach.

The GROW Coaching Model

Step	Explanation	Examples of Actual Questions to Ask
Goal	What's the goal? This is to help define what, in fact, the problem or issue is. What's the objective? What are you trying to achieve or accomplish? This can take a few minutes or quite a while, depending on what clarity the employee already has.	• What is it you would like to discuss? • What would you like to achieve? • What do you want to get from this session? • What would need to happen for you to walk away feeling that this time was well spent? • What do you want to be different? • What outcome do you want? • What would you like to happen that is not happening now? • What would you like not to happen that is happening now? • Is that realistic? • Can we do that in the time we have available? • Will that be of real value to you?

| Reality | What's the current reality or situation?

It's valuable to explore this area so the employee is very clear what is going on. This could highlight assumptions they have and gaps in knowledge – about the situation or themselves! | • What is happening at the moment?
• How do you know that this is accurate?
• When does this happen?
• How often does this happen?
• What effect does this have?
• How can you verify that this is so?
• What have you or others done previously about this?
• What other factors are relevant?
• Who else is involved?
• What is their perception of the situation?
• What have you tried so far? What did you learn? |

Options	What are the possible options? This is where you want them to brainstorm about alternatives. Continue having them generate ideas until they've reasonably exhausted the options.	• What are you thinking of doing? • What could you do to change the situation? • What alternatives are there to that approach? • Tell me what possibilities for action you see. • What approach/ actions have been used in similar circumstances? • Who might be able to help? • Would you like suggestions from me? • What are the benefits of that option? What might the problems be? • Which options are of interest to you? • Would you like to choose an option to act on?

Will or Way Forward	What's going to happen? What will you do? What's your way forward? This is the time to have the coachee define next steps and create accountability. What will they do? When? How will they ensure success?	• What are the next steps? • When will you take them? • What might get in the way? • Do you need to capture the steps in your diary? • What support do you need? • How will you enlist that support? • How will you know you are making progress? • What else needs to be done?

Don'ts:

- Don't necessarily try to complete all four steps at one time.

- Don't just focus on O and W, spend time in G and R, as so often people skim over these and later find out they were solving the wrong problem!

- Don't work so hard. Let the client/coachee/employee do the work. For example, using their actual words in your questions, pausing and being in silence so they can figure it out.

- Don't use closed questions. Use open questions that ideally start with WHAT, at least initially (WHY makes people defend what they just said, HOW focuses on doing and you might be jumping to a solution before clarifying the true problem).

- Don't use assumptive questions – a question that comes from an assumption you're making. For example: "What makes you uncomfortable about this?" Only ask this if they've told you they are uncomfortable, not if you've assumed they are. Ask them: "What are you feeling about this?"

- Don't ask leading questions – where you include possible ideas or solutions to lead the person in a certain direction. For example: "What are your plans to cut costs, reduce headcount, cancel a shift, or limit travel?" Notice you're leading them down a path, probably the typical path you would be pursuing.

- Don't answer when someone says, "I don't know." This is an easy way out for an employee especially if you've always just given the answer in the past. Either be silent to let them think or ask something like "if you did know, what would you say/do?" or "if some part of you knew, what would it say?" or "what would an expert on this say?" This line of questioning helps people find their resourcefulness within.

The How of Coaching

Coaching is more than just asking questions, listening and following a model. This is the doing of coaching – ask, listen, ask more, move to next step, wrap up with agreed actions.

There's a difference between following a recipe and being a chef and the same holds true of coaching. Partly it's the hours of practice and exposure to different ingredients and methods and partly it's the intention, mindset or beliefs they bring to the kitchen. A chef brings passion, curiosity, desire to serve, love, confidence they can transform raw ingredients and so much more.

Coaching is about how you are being while you are doing the actions. Who you are being as you coach (or do anything frankly) is a reason the opening section of this book is about you. Think about how you want to be when you coach someone – present, open, suspending judgement, attentive, open to what comes up, curious, purposeful and more. It requires dancing in the moment, having no preconceived notion of how the conversation will go, being with whatever comes up at the time.

Leaders who coach or use coaching skills with proficiency are still leaders in their organization. They wear multiple hats – leader, manager, coach, mentor, trainer, performance monitor and more. More will follow on this concept in Part 3 of the book and it's good to intentionally *choose* your coaching hat when you are coaching so that your mindset is aligned for the situation.

Top Tips:

- Use a compassionate and curious tone of voice rather than making it an interrogation.

- Acknowledge the coachee through the process, noting what they do well and how they are being during the journey (e.g. "You're open. You're reflective. You're creative. You're courageous for trying something new and unknown").

- Encourage the employee at the end of the process with their identified actions, e.g. "Those are some good actions you've identified. Go for it. You'll be great at that" (be more specific, related to the actual action).

- Champion the coachee, stand up for their potential and value, especially when they aren't feeling it, by saying what you see when they are at their best.

- Silence is good, it means someone is thinking and isn't that what you pay people for?

- Believe in yourself; at a bare minimum you at least know more about coaching than the person you are coaching.

- Practise, even if it's just asking one question, before you jump in with the solution.

THE CHALLENGE

Have a coaching conversation using the model above (or part of it) every day for the next five days.

Practise at least once a day with five different people using the full GROW model 1:1.

Try it in both your professional and personal life. For example, yesterday a friend commented to me that his teenager was "being an idiot". I asked, "Would you like to think about that comment a little?" He said "Yes." We then discussed it, with me using coaching skills. Over about three minutes I asked various questions such as "what goal do you have around that comment?", "what impact does that comment have on you?", "what could it have on him", "what perspective would you like to hold about him?" He determined that he made the comment because he was "frustrated and venting", that he felt bad "labelling" his son in that way, and that he wanted to increase his son's confidence in decision making by thinking about him as a "young buck finding his footing in a big forest".

After five days of practising coaching skills, then schedule one hour for a coaching session with a direct report. Do this once a week and make it ongoing. You can coach employees, peers, juniors in other departments. You could even coach your boss, just watch out for being patronizing.

Reflect each time you do it:

▸ What did you learn about yourself when using the model? About others?

▸ What worked well? What do you need to still practise?

- ▶ What impact did it have? Either tangible (what people said to you about it) or intangible (what you feel/sense the impact was)?

- ▶ What are the differences between telling and coaching?

- ▶ What have you noticed about other people's coaching? What works? What doesn't?

- ▶ What did you notice the first day versus the fifth, in terms of your ability/comfort?

Influence And Engage Through Storytelling

"What does storytelling have to do with people skills?", you might be thinking. A lot. As you now know, people are emotional creatures and stories are a great way of connecting with people as good storytelling is emotive. That's what makes great books and great movies: they tell engaging and emotive stories. Have you ever had feedback that you need to be more motivating or inspiring? If so, storytelling could be the answer.

In this section I'll share some reasons and benefits of storytelling. The model for storytelling is actually nine steps, to develop stories that are meaningful and powerful for you. Follow those nine steps and you'll have an array of stories that should serve you in many situations. The actual stories are the raw ingredient. How you tell or deliver the story is the recipe for making it engaging and memorable. A carrot is just a vegetable, an ingredient. Add coconut milk, earthy vegetable stock and coriander and you have a soul-warming soup. Grate it and combine it with flour, sugar, cinnamon and eggs and you have a comforting, moist cake. Slice it with onion, garlic, ginger, bok choy and soya sauce and you have a lively Asian dish.

Top Reasons People Get Scared of Storytelling

1. They think they must be entertaining

2. They think they need to be an actor and deliver a script eloquently

3. They think they are not creative

4. They worry about being put on the spot

5. They think it's about speaking in public, like a presentation

6. They are worried about looking stupid or silly

7. They are worried about appearing vulnerable or making a mistake

Benefits of Storytelling

- You appeal to someone's emotions

- You share part of yourself with others, to connect personally

- You make a point in an entertaining or descriptive way

- You show flexibility in communication style thereby being more relatable to different people

The What of Storytelling

Want to hear the secret of storytelling? It's about thinking of your stories before you might even need or want to share them. That's right, plan them in advance. The process is the same for your professional or personal stories, depending on your audience; however, here the focus is on professional. It's not as complicated as the following nine steps imply. I've just broken it down in detail to walk you through the process step-by-step.

1. Peak moments – Think about your professional journey, what have been the highlights, low points, key lessons learned and crossroads. Also, think about what matters to you as a leader and where that purpose or motivation came from. If you're struggling, think of some things you'd like a graduate to know about leadership and try and remember where you learned that lesson in your career personally.

2. Your situation – From the specific events and moments in time identified above, think about your situation – your thoughts, feelings, motivations and relationships with those involved in each of those peak moments.

3. Lessons – Identify the lessons you learned from each of those peak moments. In other words, what is the moral of each of your peak moments? This will become the 'so what' of your story and be useful in identifying which story to share and when to share it, so stay tuned.

4. Choose – Which topics or morals might be the most applicable to your current leadership situation? Which might be helpful to the challenges your team members are facing now?

5. Create – Take the topic or moral from above and create the story, including the situation, the learning moment, the feelings and the 'so what' or moral.

6. Elaborate – Put in more emotion (you probably have skimped on feelings as so many people do), share the angst and the light bulb feeling, include specific details to add flavour and paint a picture, and lastly, reveal how that transformed or impacted you from that moment on.

7. Refine – Delete some of the factual filler or extra words. The length of your story should be about 3 to 5 minutes. You could have a slightly longer version depending on the application.

8. Practise – by yourself. First read it over and feel it. Then read it out loud to hear yourself say it (you don't want the first time you hear it to be when another hears it). Then read it in front of a mirror, occasionally looking at your face in the mirror. This increases your comfort level further. Hone the message and wording, if necessary.

9. Deliver – This isn't about memorizing a story, it's about knowing the structure and flow of what you want to convey. Try it out with a low-risk person and use your newfound awareness-sensing skills to judge the impact. Or you could ask for feedback! Also, watch how others tell stories – what works and what doesn't for them.

The way to use your stories practically is to have a small inventory of 3–5 in your mind to use when the situation warrants. For example, when a colleague says to you they are struggling to give needed feedback to one of their team, tell them the story (which you've already prepared) of when you had that same situation and what you learned (in addition to showing them the feedback chapter in this book). Or if one of your employees made a visible (but not a gross) mistake, share your story of when your mistake was your biggest growth opportunity and how it improved your performance dramatically. Sharing your story is a way of motivating and inspiring people in difficult situations to excel.

Anthony's Case Study Example – Identifying and Lessons for Storytelling

A senior client, I'll call him Anthony, with a huge, dispersed team came to a recent session quite upset. He was reeling with the amount of stress, burnout and agitation within his broader team. The trigger event had been the suicide of a team member lower down in the organization. The employee's family reassured the team that the suicide had been unrelated to work. The company immediately put support mechanisms in place for all employees. Despite the reassurances and resources, the energy among the team was troubled. My client was worried about his people – wanting them to know that their health and wellbeing were not worth sacrificing for anything. The care and conviction in his voice was profound. As I started probing what was going on for him, words stopped, and emotion started breaking through. He was connecting to a time, years earlier, when he was driving himself into the ground due to work pressure. He learned back then that the pressure was self-imposed, it was his self-doubt, worry of the future and unrealistic expectations that were harming him more than what his boss was demanding. When he talked about how he came through it, arresting it before burning out, the message for his people became clear. From our discussion he would share his experience from this sensitive, empathetic perspective.

The How of Storytelling

Authentic, impactful storytelling comes from your heart. It's your expression of your experiences. It shows your foibles, your passion and your self-reflection. Where people so often go wrong is that they try and make up an inspiring story; that's fabrication not authenticity. They also strip out the emotions and context to communicate the facts, transforming a story into a patronizing one-line instruction such as, "I once missed a crucial deadline too and learned from it so now I ensure key stakeholders are engaged well beforehand." Or for Anthony's story above it would be "I once almost experienced burnout and learned to pace myself and not neglect looking after myself." They could have read that in a book for the amount of inspiration it conveys.

Feel it – tell the story remembering and feeling the emotions of the time you are talking about. Feel the tiredness and relentless pressure you felt when approaching burnout (if we're referencing Anthony's story) and then the relief and self-compassion of coming out the other side.

Pace – change the pace during your story, use pauses, make eye contact, breathe. These things create variety for the listener, allow the emotion to come through and keep you present in the story rather than 'just recounting the story' as if memorized.

Tone of voice – what's your usual tone of voice? What adjectives would you use to describe how you communicate – Funny? Colloquial? Polite? Chatty? Authoritative? Energizing? Expert? Reflective? Factual? I describe my tone of voice as direct and succinct.

I was part of a book writing group when I wrote this book, led by an awesome book coach, Alison Jones,[1] who gave us the exercise to write in different tones of voice. That exercise allowed me to communicate in different voices and recognize when to switch between different tones for variety and emphasis. Also, writing in different voices helped me realize key messages that were missing from my original communication. I include the tone of voice exercise I did while writing the first paragraph of Principle 3 on feedback as an example for you to experiment with your tone of voice and when to change it as needed.

1. Original

   Giving feedback is a great place to start the OUTSIDE section. It is about putting your attention on another person – a team member, employee, peer or even boss – noticing the other person's behaviours, qualities and/or results. And then actually communicating those specific observations to that individual for their growth, and that's getting ahead of ourselves.

2. Emotional

   Giving feedback is an exciting and scary place to start the OUTSIDE section of the book. We leave behind the safe and familiar world of the "self" and move to the unknown of "other(s)" which might make you anxious and uncertain. Or inspired and playful about putting your attention on another – a frustrating team member, happy employee, a peer or even your confident boss – noticing the other person's rich tapestry of behaviours, qualities and/or results.

And then you are communicating those specific observations bravely, and let's take one tiny step at a time.

3. Motivational

   You'll see that giving feedback is the simplest and most impactful place to start the OUTSIDE section of the book. It's such an exciting thing to focus on other people, whether a team member, employee, peer or even boss. Imagine what it would be like for you to confidently give and receive feedback for their growth. Armed with an idea of how to notice another person's behaviours, qualities and/or results and have the courage provided by a framework to communicate it, you've got feedback nailed!

4. Instructional

   Now we start the OUTSIDE section of the book by covering feedback. You will be taught what to notice in other people's behaviours, qualities and/or results and how to communicate positive or negative feedback to them so they improve.

5. Personal

   Giving feedback is the place I want to point you to at the start of the OUTSIDE section of the book. This is an area many clients struggle with, from thinking 'good job' was enough to praise them, to not knowing what to do to deal positively with others who were not as effective as they could have been. This topic will help you understand that feedback is about being in service to someone else by noticing their behaviours, qualities and/or results in the first place and then productively communicating that to them for their growth.

6. Shocking

   If you only get one thing out of this book, feedback should be it! It's about getting over yourself and your own insecurities and caring more about other people and their growth. It starts with paying attention to others, something we forget when we're uncertain of ourselves or scared, and then communicating simple improvements to that person in a structured way.

THE CHALLENGE

Go through the nine steps above to create two stories in the next week. Just pick the first two most memorable moments in your career journey if you're struggling.

Try it in both your professional and personal life. For example, when people ask me what brought me to live in London, I could easily answer "my uncle, who lived here, suggested it". True, and boring and tells you nothing about me personally. Instead, the story I tell (after working through this process myself) illustrates my belief in saying YES to the unknown and trusting what comes along. My answer to why I live in London is:

The universe picked it. On a sunny, Sunday afternoon in Switzerland my uncle, who had lived in London for over 50 years, called me and asked "Do you know where you're going to live next?" as he knew my then-husband and I were going to be leaving Switzerland in the next three months. I replied "no", which was the truth, my soon-to-be-ex was moving back to Canada and Canada wasn't calling me back. My uncle asked "Have you thought of living in London?" I said "Of course I have, but where would I start?" He didn't know at the time that my marriage was ending. He suggested "Well, I want to move back to Canada and the only thing stopping me is my flat and my furnishings. So, if you buy my flat and furnishings and move to London I'll move to Canada?" In shock, I stammered, "Really, I've never heard you talk of going back to Canada?" "Yes", he said, he's a man of few words. "Can I afford your flat?" I tentatively inquired, knowing I'd be buying it on my own as a single woman just starting my own business, which was scary. "We'll make sure you can, friends and family discount." To which I replied "Well, I guess I'm moving to London." "Sorted", he concluded. "Great, we'll talk more." I gasped in disbelief. And with that five-minute conversation I was moving to London.

This story takes me about 90 seconds to 2 minutes to share (I can talk quickly), with pauses, genuineness of the fear, disbelief and excitement I felt at the time. I've shared that story many times, as people are always curious about a foreigner in their midst, and I have received feedback that it's inspiring and I'm courageous or brave.

Deliver at least one story to at least one person in the next week. Repeat.

Bonus task: Take two sentences from your story and write them in four different tones of voice. Which feel comfortable for you and which are a stretch? When would it be worthwhile to use another tone of voice in your story to have more impact?

Reflect each time you do it:

▸ What did you learn about yourself when using the nine-step process?

▸ What worked well? What do you need to still practise?

▸ What impact did delivering the story have? Either tangible (what people said to you about it) or intangible (what you feel/sense the impact was)?

▸ What are the differences when you share stories?

▸ What have you noticed about other people's storytelling? What works? What doesn't?

▸ What did you notice the first day versus the fifth, in terms of your ability/comfort with both the process and delivery?

BONUS PART 2 CHALLENGE

If you're very advanced or up for a double challenge, then you could think about some of the things in Part 1 INSIDE that you learned about yourself and practise the positive angles of those traits with the models and tips from the OUTSIDE section. For example: if you know that you're like me and tend to be quick and efficient, practise slowing down, when using any of the tips of feedback, coaching or storytelling. This hints a bit to Part 3 as well – the balance BETWEEN the INSIDE and OUTSIDE.

PART 3

BETWEEN

This is the hardest Part, I think. And maybe it's hard because I think it is. It's the dance between yourself and another person. It's the valley between two mountain peaks. It's the space between the sun and the moon. It's the energy field between two magnets. It's the gulf between the North and South Rims of the Grand Canyon. It's the river between opposing sandbanks. And it can be opposite sides of the same coin... a fine line... a razor and a whisker... two peas in a pod... identical/monozygotic twins.

Given you're reading this book, you are responsible for navigating this space between you and another person. If you are already close to that other person, great. If not, imagine you are on one side of a river and the other person is on the other side. What are the possibilities between the two of you? The water, the air, rocks, a bridge, a shout, a boat, a helicopter, really long arms... the list is endless. And I always suggest to clients that you are responsible for building the bridge between yourself and the other person. You must walk towards them over that bridge until they are ready to meet you on the bridge or come to your side. You might be lucky and have them trot over and meet you part way. Rarely will they teleport themselves to your side instantaneously. We are all guilty of living our lives from our own perspectives, seeing the world through our own eyes and acting in our own interests. And other people live their lives the same way. It's amazing in some ways that we ever connect.

This Part of the book is about navigating between your INSIDE self and other people in the OUTSIDE world.

The thinking behind this Part is the notion, often attributed to Aristotle, that the whole is greater than the sum of the parts. Or as Stephen Gilligan and Robert Dilts share in their book, *The Hero's Journey*, when explaining the idea of the 'field', the space around individuals: "if you combine two hydrogen atoms and an oxygen atom you get something rather astonishing. You get water, which is neither hydrogen nor oxygen."[1] The BETWEEN is the uniqueness you bring, the uniqueness the other person brings, and the magic result of the intermingling of those two entities.

This Part will cover adapting, balancing and exposing.

First, we will cover adapting yourself to other people, the situation and the desired outcomes. I'll start with the benefits of adapting for everyone involved, the benefits for you, the other person and the organization as well. Then I'll get into the meat of how to adapt rather than comply or impose. The question of manipulation will be addressed, from the perspective of whether influencing others by adapting yourself is manipulation. The concepts of experimentation and play are shared to make adapting easier to try. A list of tips and a case study are included to aid your comprehension.

Second, balancing will visually illustrate all the different elements that need to be balanced when interacting with others, depending on the situation. This doesn't mean they have to be used equally, it is about modulating between two extremes as appropriate. Unfortunately, there is no cut and dried rule, it varies. Imagine walking on a tightrope (a bad analogy as it could imply a somewhat precarious endeavour), how you perform (another bad analogy as this isn't about you performing, rather being authentic) is influenced by the height of the rope off the ground; the wind and visibility; whether you fear heights or not; the importance of tightrope-walking to you; the prize upon completion, if any; and how skilled you are at it. And the most important thing once you're on the rope is being present, in the moment, putting one foot in front of the other.

Lastly, this section will cover the unusual and potentially off-putting topics of vulnerability and courage – cue uneasiness. Sorry. They really go hand in hand and are required for high performance, especially in leadership. A firefighter can't be courageous entering a burning building without making him or herself vulnerable to death, harm, making a mistake that costs someone their life or needing to be rescued by their colleagues if things go terribly wrong.

PRINCIPLE 6

Adapt Authentically To Others And The Situation

A dapting authentically is about how you navigate that space between you and another person with whom you are in contact, in a way that still allows you to be you and to achieve what you want to achieve. First, this assumes you need and/or want to be in contact with this other person. In the context of this book you probably need them in some way to achieve your goal or the organization's objective(s). Second, you know you are different from the other person, with differing perspectives, inter-relational preferences, personalities and objectives. And since you are the one reading this book, you are responsible for managing your interaction with them. Lastly, this isn't about you conforming to their needs and wishes or changing who you are; it's about you *being* who you are with all your uniqueness while interacting. As I said earlier, this is about being yourself with more skill. It's too much work and energy to be someone you aren't, so I suggest striving to be your better self.

Benefits of Adapting Authentically

1. To You:
    a. You get to be yourself and do not have to wear a mask or put on an act

    b. It focuses your energy on the relationship and the business

    c. It feels like you are in your own skin, being yourself

2. To Others:

    a. They are truly seen as individuals and unique beings

    b. They have a role model that it's OK to be yourself

    c. They know who you are authentically, making it easier to predict how you'll be

3. To the Organization:

    a. Less energy conforming to a mythical way of being

    b. A positive place where people are encouraged to be themselves

    c. More efficient and productive as people build bridges rather than staking out their own territories

    d. A more agile organization as people are aware of how they are being in relationships, not just interacting

Isn't Adapting Really Complying?

The *Oxford English Dictionary* definition of adapting is: "make (something) suitable for a new use or purpose; modify. Become adjusted to new conditions."

Complying is one means of adapting oneself when interacting with another person, as is mimicking or confronting. Adapting, when it comes to building a relationship, using soft skills and wanting to achieve business objectives, is subtler or more nuanced than just copying or complying. Adapting is about being intentional in the way you interact with the other person.

Adapting is easy when you're dealing with someone like you. You both share similar views and values; preferences for particular styles of communication, decision making; your work objectives are aligned. It's much harder when the other person is different or even your polar opposite. My last boss was very unlike me, we often contradicted each other, and we had competing approaches and priorities, despite having the same objectives. Initially I was frustrated and ineffective until I reframed how I viewed our differences. Rather than being contradictory or competing, I labelled us complementary and, hence, exceptionally compatible because we covered the spectrum rather than just one part of it! I adapted my mindset first when approaching her and then adapted my interaction to see our differences as valuable and worthy of exploration.

Complementary	vs	Competing
Compatible	vs	Contradictory

Tips on How to Adapt Authentically

Although it's hard to be prescriptive about how to be in relationship with another person, there are some tips to increase your comfort and likelihood of success.

1. Know yourself – this is so you are conscious of your preferences, values, default habits, communication style, what you are bringing to the interaction.

2. Know the other person as best you can – being curious about what they are thinking, and feeling, is very helpful for you to know the other half of the dynamic. Coaching skills are useful here to learn about the other person by inquiring without interrogating. The more often you interact with someone, the more you could learn about them; start to create a picture of them that parallels the information you have about yourself.

3. Be aware of the situation you find yourself in or that you are trying to create – in emotional intelligence language this is called **social awareness.**

   i.   What do you want to achieve?

   ii. What are the needs and wants of the other person?

   iii. What are your feelings in this moment?

   iv. What are the feelings of the other person right now?

   v.   What are the stressors in terms of topic or time that might impact things?

   vi. Are you on the same side or opposite sides of the river or on the bridge together?

4. Start the exchange.

   i.   Start by checking you know where each of you is relative to the river (topic). "What I wanted to talk about is..." or "The objective for this conversation is..." or "I want to touch base on..."

ii. Give context – leaders give **context** rather than just focusing on the **content.** Leaders don't assume people know where they are coming from or why they are asking for whatever they are asking for. They take the time to share the WHY for the task, or ask rather than just saying what they want. Sharing a common context helps to get you both on the same side of the river or on the bridge together.

iii. Check if they are on the same page as you – ask them *"I want to make sure I'm being clear, what are you taking from what I am sharing?"* This puts the responsibility for being clear on you, rather than asking them if they understand. Asking them if they understand could imply it's their fault if they don't get it rather than it being your fault you didn't communicate it well. Since you're the one reading the book, you take responsibility for your clarity and communication rather than blaming their comprehension. (If it's a pattern of them not getting it, that's a different conversation – a worthwhile one).

iv. Respond to what they say; remember, respond, not react. As Stephen Covey brilliantly said decades ago in *The 7 Habits of Highly Effective People*: "Seek first to understand then to be understood."[1] That means listening to understand what they are saying, checking in that you understand what they've said, where they are coming from, what their perspective is, before putting forward your opinion and trying to be understood by them.

v. Be You

vi. Repeat

Holly's Case Study Example – Adapting Authentically

I had a client with two bosses – one direct line manager and the other a dotted line manager. Both were essential to her career progression and success in the role. These two managers could not have been more different, their only real similarity was they were both male – one liked detail and the other adored big picture; one held control over decisions and the other preferred my client to make all the decisions; one demanded frequent communication and the other only wanted contact as needed. My client needed to adapt her approach when dealing with these different managers to be successful, to be respected, to get support and for everyone to enjoy their interaction. To figure out how to maximize her relationships with these two bosses we started with her (that's why Part 1 INSIDE of the book is Part 1), for her to know herself and what was authentically her. Then she analyzed her two managers to understand as much about them as she could (she essentially did as much of Part 1 INSIDE on each of them as she could without being them). It was this analysis of them that helped her really understand the differences between them and be clear on what each of them preferred in terms of interaction. We then determined when in her life she is detailed/hands on/in control and where she is big picture/hands off/ empowering. With a new and shaky member of her team she was hands on and detail oriented, she checked in and followed up, she asked lots of questions and dissected options. With her husband and their home renovations she was hands off and big picture, leaving him to handle most of it, with her just focused on the final outcome. By seeing and feeling those differences within herself she could tap into them as appropriate to be authentic when dealing with the respective managers.

Another idea for adapting authentically is a concept often taught in improvization comedy (or improv). It's based on the idea that in an improv comedy show, you want to make your fellow actor look good by receiving whatever they throw your way. It's to say "YES, AND". Finding something in what the other person is saying or doing that you can agree with and building on it. In improv theatre they must do this because if they refused what was suggested the skit could just go back and forth with "no, this", "no, this", "no, this" and not be entertaining. You could even say "What I like about that is..." to emphasize that you are taking something from what they shared and creating from it. A similar idea is the 2% truth – find 2% of truth in what the other person brings to the discussion and build from there. This is a much more collaborative approach and more motivating for the other person than having their entire contribution dismissed. And *find* the 2% truth for you, don't make it up, that's not genuine or authentic.

Here's an example from a retail operation that I overheard while typing this section:

Manager Case Study Example – YES, AND

A store manager digitally modified some signage provided by marketing head office. When he showed it to the marketing manager, she wasn't happy with the fact he had done it as it wasn't as professional as the solution her team had provided. She responded really well by asking "what was behind you needing to do that?" He said, "I need to be able to react quickly to some themes going on in my local area, so the communication is more relevant." After a (luckily) brief complaint that it wasn't professional and against the brand guidelines, she offered to see if the department could give him a template to use in the future. If she had been using the YES, AND she could have said "YES I see your need to localize and act fast AND let me see how we could provide you with a template and software to do that."

Some clients have asked "isn't this manipulation?" The *Oxford English Dictionary* defines manipulate as: "handle or control (a tool, mechanism, information, etc.) in a skilful manner. Control or influence (a person or situation) cleverly or unscrupulously." So, yes, it is manipulation. And, so what? If you get what you want while being yourself AND the other person is treated well, with full permission to say 'yes' or 'no', and has their needs met, what does it matter? The issue is the intention behind the interaction; if it's to influence for good reasons, then OK; if it's to influence for unscrupulous, evil, bad reasons, then it's not.

Play and Experiment

Language can have a powerful impact on a person's attitude and receptivity – your own or someone else's. Clients often tell me they "have to have a difficult conversation" with one of their employees and want support in how to do that. If they feel it's going to be a difficult conversation, it probably will be. I start by asking how they'd like it to be – and the choices can be "fun, productive, beneficial, encouraging, empowering, and stimulating", to name a few. How about expressing it as wanting to have a conversation with an employee to clarify expectations and create mutual understanding? I also have them reflect on the words "need to have or should have or have to have a conversation". This implies that it's probably a discussion that's overdue, if not long overdue. So in addition to the importance of language, they should probably do it sooner, rather than later.

My ex-husband said he hated it when I said, "we need to talk" (remember this was before I was more aware). I was usually at the end of my tether when I said this, almost like some imaginary line of 'too much' had been crossed. I've now learned to just share what I'm thinking or feeling at the first sign or two of me feeling uneasy, no matter the sensitivity of the topic, and ask my partner to help me sort out what's going on for me and how to solve it. Imagine instead if I had said "I need your help figuring out some anxiety I'm having, do you have time to help now?" People like to help others, hence me asking for his help. I also frame it as a problem with me, which it is, rather than making him wrong or blaming him.

What does that language preamble have to do with Adapting Authentically? Embrace the language of playing and experimentation to practise adapting authentically. Make it fun. Be OK with trying it out rather than trying to be perfect. Playing has no right or wrong outcome; it's the state of being in the moment of enjoyment. It's the same for experimentation; it's about testing theories and discovering new things. As Thomas A. Edison said, "I have not failed. I've just found 10,000 ways that won't work." At a conference of young entrepreneurs in their early twenties presenting their ideas for businesses with social conscience, the word 'pivot' was used to describe the evolution or progress of their endeavour. When they came to an impasse, barrier or obstacle in their process, they just pivoted. They just took that point not as failure or termination, simply as a need to head in another direction, pursue another angle or possibility. That's what I'm suggesting for you. Try something – asking a question you usually wouldn't, giving context that might seem obvious to you, checking in with the other person – and if it falls flat, check in, name it or change tack. You may find that the other person is surprised by your new actions and behaviours, so, if it falls flat, this could just be because they are surprised or uncertain about what's going on. You can name it if you want, for example: "I'm trying out some new communication concepts which might not be working right now. I'm trying to give you some context or the reason why before sharing the task. How could I do that more effectively?" Alternatively, just try it a few times with that person to see if they shift in terms of their receptivity. You've had time to digest new and different ideas, give them time to do the same.

Experiment and Play with:

- Who – start with lower risk individuals such as people with whom you are less emotionally charged. A host at a restaurant and wait-staff or service providers are readily available and low risk as you probably won't ever see them again. People you're talking to on the phone are good opportunities as well. Kids are always up for playing, follow their lead.

- What – you, them, between, values, feelings, preferences in communication, strengths, giving context, empowering language, intention going into the interaction, curiosity, open questions, pausing, slowing down, silence, where are each of you relative to the river, pivot.

- When – pre-emptive or earlier in the interaction rather than when there's an entrenched issue. Often and now.

Part of the playing is not just to figure out the other person and how to adapt, it's also about figuring out who you are authentically. Play with who you are, especially when you are at your best, and who you strive to be, that consistently better version of yourself.

THE CHALLENGE

Enter into a conversation today with the goal to adapt your interaction with another person authentically to achieve something that you need done. Try at least one authentic adaptation per day for five days.

Notice other people in terms of authenticity and adjusting – who are they when they are being authentic? How do they adapt themselves to other people? This can be people you work with, those in the news or characters in a movie or show. Watch the dance between the two; where is each of them positioned relative to the river, and who is moving towards the other thereby building the bridge, and who isn't? You can learn as much from watching someone resisting or being overbearing as you can from someone dancing effortlessly.

Think of people you interact with regularly and start building a profile of what their preferences are and what their needs and wants are. It's great to start with your boss, your partner and some key stakeholders.

After five days of playing or experimenting, sit down and reflect on the practice.

Reflect each time you do it:

▶ What did you learn about yourself from adapting authentically? About others?

▶ What worked well? What do you need to still practise?

▶ What impact did you have? Either tangible (what people said to you about it) or intangible (what you feel/sense the impact was).

▸ What are the differences between playing and performing?

▸ What have you noticed about other people's authentic adaptation? What works? What doesn't?

▸ What did you notice the first day versus the fifth, in terms of your ability/comfort?

Human Interaction Is A Balancing Act

Human interactions are, by definition, complicated. It's an interaction or a dance between two distinct people. At the same time as you're dancing with another there's also a dance with yourself – of your emotions, thoughts, sensations. And the other person has their own dance going on within themselves too. We don't suspend our thoughts, feelings, views, experiences or personal growth opportunities when we interact with another person and neither do they. How you show up (behaviour and intention) in that interaction with someone else is the only real thing you can control or influence, at least initially.

You're smart. You have great experience, decades of working under your belt, you've been promoted a few times and hope for a couple more promotions before you retire. You've been successful so far in your career and you've probably accomplished in your personal life too. A lot of that success has come from hard work, putting in the hours, getting the work done and pushing yourself. Who am I to say you should tamper with that winning formula? Or maybe someone in your organization has said you need to change or at least soften around the edges?

The Balance Principle is not about throwing out everything that's enabled you to get where you are today. Not at all. Rather it's about taking all those good things and adding some complementary ideas, behaviours and actions to be even more well-rounded. It's about adding tools to your toolbox. If you want to cut down a tree, a hammer is not much help, whereas a chainsaw, crosscut saw, axe or pruning shears give you many options depending on the situation. If we hold with the dance metaphor, the more dances you know (waltz, foxtrot, salsa, Macarena, floss), the more potential partners you'll have and the more possibilities for dancing. The same with skills for success, especially as you advance upwards in an organization. A senior leader needs to have an understanding of all the functional areas like Finance, Operations, HR, Compliance, Marketing, Research, etc., to increase their likelihood of success. The same is true of their soft skills; the broader a leader's knowledge of interacting with different people, the greater their success.

What Is Balance?

Balance is about having things in the correct proportion, so the overall mix is stable rather than lopsided or unbalanced. Imagine a seesaw or teeter-totter, both sides need to have similar weight for the game to work, to have fun. Otherwise one end just goes bang to the ground and the game's over. It isn't about equality or exactly equal parts.

For the arena of soft skills, the interaction between two or more people, we've already discussed telling versus listening. The Principle of balance is about recognizing that you need to have a balance between the skills of telling and listening that's appropriate to the situation and people involved. Balance is about increasing your range of people skills so that you can use them in the doses you need to increase your effectiveness. Balance is about the right proportions for the given circumstances. Maybe it helps to think about it more as a continuum, with listening at one end and telling at the other. Some situations warrant all listening (a colleague's child is gravely ill), some warrant all telling (there's a fire, EVACUATE IMMEDIATELY!), and most situations are somewhere in between – the vital thing is to pick from the broad range in between the extreme ends.

The Listening Telling Scale

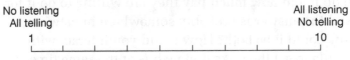

Where is the ideal point on the continuum given the situation?

The key is finding the right balance between different skills within yourself and balancing those with the individual and situation in front of you in the moment.

What to Balance

As you've established in the previous Parts, you have natural tendencies or preferences that you exhibit when interacting with someone. Sometimes, given the person or situation, you might be more effective if you balanced those tendencies with some other behaviours. If you're very analytical all the time, you might want to balance that with narrative storytelling for variety or to appeal to non-analytical people. Here is a list of things to practise balancing to increase your repertoire of tools in your toolbox.

1. What and How

Most of your focus at work is on getting the work done and getting your people to get the work done – whether that's bringing in new business, running the distribution operations for a large national retailer, overseeing all the IT systems for a multinational, or leading product development for the next decade. You need to get tasks done and enable other people to get tasks done. How you interact with other people to get those tasks done can vary significantly. You can be a dictator and just tell them what to do and how to do it. You can be a nanny and ask them what they'd like to do and how they'd like to do it and when they'd like to do it and how much pay they are willing to do it for. And the answer is probably somewhere in between; how could it be both? How could you interact with people to get the tasks done *while* at the same time at least maintaining, if not growing, the relationship with them? That's the ultimate balance – to **balance the soft skills and hard results so they can co-exist together.**

When you are in a new situation or have a new team member or maybe you have a new boss, it's often beneficial to build the relationship as a priority while doing the work. Many clients with new team members or bosses start the interaction with a project review meeting where the status of all the work is shared. This is important because you are paid to deliver results and your new boss is probably paid more to deliver more results. Through coaching, my clients often come to realize that most success (or failure) hinges on the relationship, so some priority needs to be given to the relationship itself. The first session in any 1:1 coaching I run includes 'designing the alliance' – what work will

we do together and how do we want to 'be' together –
what brings out the best in each of us? Designing the
alliance is an overt discussion about the goals, roles and
ways of interacting for mutual enjoyment and client
success. For example, for me to be at my best and make
the coaching the best for my client I need permission
from them to interrupt. I'm not being rude, it's just that
I need less of the 'story' about what is happening than
they think I need, my focus is on the 'so what?', what
matters to them in this story. This honours my value of
efficiency and allows them to get the most out of our
time together, more bang for their buck (or pound or
euro)! If I hadn't told them I'd interrupt they might feel
hurt, rushed, that I wasn't listening, apologetic, wrong,
none of which are true or helpful. By overtly agreeing
how we work together we can then monitor how we are
doing throughout the coaching relationship; if something
doesn't feel right, we have permission to discuss it as we
agreed the ground rules at the start. You can download
my 'design the alliance' worksheet/template from my
website at www.directions-coaching.com/ as it's good for
using with colleagues and team members to explicitly
talk about how best to work together.

Balancing the WHAT and HOW

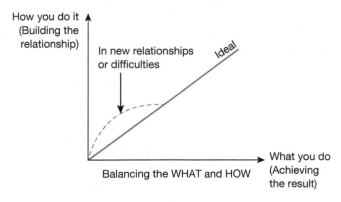

Balancing the WHAT and HOW

'What' or Task-Focused Behaviours

These are things you can do to manage tasks well:

- Doing it yourself
- Dictating the methodology of how to do it, directing
- Defining accountability
- Monitoring progress
- Setting KPIs (key performance indicators), goals, objectives, targets
- Having timelines/deadlines
- Evaluating, analyzing
- Making decisions
- Following up, control
- Identifying road blocks and barriers
- Delegating
- Reporting status, updates, facts
- Managing risk
- Measuring, allocating
- Taking corrective action

'How' or Relationship-Oriented Behaviours

These are behaviours that you can use to manage people well and build the relationship with them:

- Trying to understand
- Being interested
- Having empathy
- Collaborating
- Looking after people
- Giving and taking feedback
- Celebrating success, appreciating
- Learning from mistakes
- Coaching
- Sharing the purpose, the why
- Listening, really listening
- Inspiring, engaging
- Creating and communicating vision
- Joking, laughing, humour
- Emitting charisma
- Showing yourself, being vulnerable
- Talking about feelings and emotions
- Being present, taking time with people
- Supporting and defending people, having their back
- Including others
- Sensing, guiding, trusting in others
- Empowering

2. Context and Content

Context is the idea of explaining the bigger picture to people, giving them context for the work they are doing. It is the frame within which they paint. Often it can be the organizational vision or goals that necessitate certain work or tasks to be done. It is the 'why' behind the 'what' people are doing. It helps people understand why they are doing what they are doing; whereas **content** is the specific work, actions or tasks that need to be done. It's the day-to-day work; the 'what' that needs to be accomplished. Context doesn't have to be as lofty as the corporate vision, it could be as simple as why you're asking or saying what you're saying. An analogy for this is particles and space. The particles are the details or specifics and the space is the environment in which those particles sit. Imagine a status meeting about a specific project. The particles are the location, time, agenda items, the status of each action item. The space is why the meeting is even happening in the first place, the purpose of the discussion, the ambition for the project and why it's important.

This concept has been an eye-opener for me; I'm so comfortable with particles/details that I forget other people aren't in my head to see where the particles fit in the bigger picture. I was leading a group to facilitate better remote communication between them. They were trying to decide how often to have virtual calls to share their progress on each of their personal goals. They had been struggling with the size of the group, wanting different frequency of communication and were concerned they'd be forced into something they didn't want and would overtly resist. There was frustration and aggression amongst the group and defiance by one person who remained seated with her arms crossed. I had each person place their name on a bullseye image on a flipchart with the centre of the bullseye labelled 'frequently' and the outer ring of five rings labelled 'sporadically'. After the break, I broke them into three groups based on where they put their names on the bullseye. There was confusion, irritation and pushback of why they were allocated to the group they were in; I had failed to mention that I'd grouped them according to where they put themselves on the bullseye. It seemed obvious to me *and* I hadn't linked it to the flipchart exercise. Once I explained that context, they were happy they were with like-minded individuals. Then I gave them the content, "Decide in your small group how you want to communicate amongst yourselves." They easily and happily created their own schedule for meeting – date, time, means, topic, minutes – they were excited and totally committed as it was entirely their decision. Each group then shared what they agreed with the other groups, and two people changed groups as another group's schedule appealed to them more. The whole group then effortlessly decided the mechanism for communicating between the resulting three groups.

Balancing the Context/Space and Content/Particles

What's the ideal ratio given the situation?

3. Being and Doing

We are human BEINGS! You wouldn't know it given how much we DO in our lives – work, family, exercise, fun activities, social media, DIY, reading, playing with the kids, commuting, laundry, shopping, friends, checking emails, sleeping, showering, meditating, sex, holidays, preparing meals, eating, celebrating, errands, going to the doctor, overseeing homework, gardening, peeing, planning, banking... I could go on and on and you get the idea.

Mindfulness, meditation, intentionality and spirituality now have increased presence in mass/popular media, entering everyday vernacular. There are a proliferation of books, courses, apps and articles about the 'being' element of living. Business schools are even offering courses on meditation. The state of being is a quality, your essence as you are in the moment, not a goal or achievement. Being happy is a state, not a goal. The balance suggested here is how to BE as you DO. How you are being impacts how you feel and what others feel interacting with you and how successful you can be. Here's a scenario to illustrate: What if your boss has called you frantically asking for an analysis of the recent figures for a request by a C-suite member. When delegating that request to your analyst which state of being would be most effective:

a. Rushed, stressed, needy?

b. Engaging, efficient, clear?

c. Directive, thorough, serious?

It depends, b or c are both possible answers. It depends on the analyst – are they experienced and reliable or new and uncertain? The former would probably respond best to you being engaging and efficient because they are confident they can do the task with the required urgency. The latter would probably appreciate you being directive and serious, so they are sure they do it right and they understand the importance of the task, and you'd feel more confident it was done well given their newness.

Last year when I started writing this book I had a series of health issues, nothing catastrophic – enough to impact my daily life. One of my issues was pneumonia. It knocked me out. I wasn't hospitalized and I focused on doing client-only work and nothing more. Bedrest and couch time were my priority – partly because I couldn't physically do anything else. During this time, I was co-leading a project for a leadership course I was taking (not giving) and having additional weekly calls with a small group of fellow participants on other reading and homework that was required. I learned over those two months that sometimes just *being* is enough. I showed up for the calls having done no preparation, which was so unlike me. My historic pattern had been to do lots of pre-work, figure it all out, have all the questions answered and identify any areas I wanted to discuss further. Very much DOING, and mostly on my own. Pneumonia forced me to just BE – I showed up for the call, listened, learned, contributed what I could, was focused and very much leaned into the group (partly for their energy). Also, because it took all my energy just to be on the call, I was more present, less distracted and not multi-tasking by thinking of other things. I learned a great deal because I was open and receptive to others' ideas. The feedback was that my contribution was valuable, even when I was just thinking in the moment and not because of all the pre-work! It was easier and richer than what I had experienced previously when I was just DOING it.

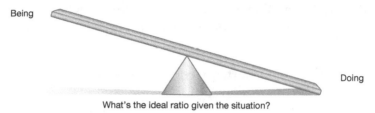

Balancing the BEING and DOING

Being

Doing

What's the ideal ratio given the situation?

4. Head and Heart

There is the balance between thinking and feeling, the emotional and intellectual, both for you and others. How are you feeling in a given moment? What are you thinking? And the same for those with whom you interact – how are they feeling and what are they thinking? This acknowledges that both **emotions** and **thoughts** are present all the time and, in fact, thoughts and feelings ultimately frame everything about how we see our life. In our work life we tend to prioritize the head, wanting solutions that are smart and fact-based. We often dismiss the importance of emotions in decision making. Often, we will have a gut-feeling or sense of what should be done and then we seek data to confirm our hunch (unconsciously in many cases). This is called *confirmation bias*. That's why it's important to be aware of both thoughts and feelings to ensure we're 'seeing' all the information and not just what we want to see.

Intuition can seem like a touchy-feely concept; a bit too woo-woo for a serious business person. Neuroscientists are discovering that there may be a scientific basis for intuition or gut-feel. The longest cranial nerve in the body is called the vagus nerve. It originates in the abdomen and is in contact with all the major organs such as intestines, stomach, liver, spleen, gallbladder, lungs and heart, before entering the brain stem. The vagus nerve transmits sensory information between the gut and brain passing by these major organs. The theory is that what we call intuition or having a gut-feeling is actual stimulation of the vagus nerve from some part of our core being transmitted to our brain. So there appears to be increasing fact-based information to justify listening to your intuition.[1]

Balancing Head/Intellectual and Heart/Emotional

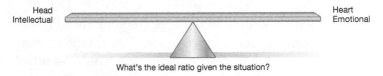

What's the ideal ratio given the situation?

5. Left and Right Brain Hemispheres

You are probably starting to see the similarities among the various elements to be balanced.

The left hemisphere controls the right side of the body. As stated previously, the left-brain functions are logic, reasoning, analytical, language, written, detail, moving things forward and numbers. The right brain controls the left side of the body and is associated more with arts, creativity, music, holistic view, intuition, visual, deeper meaning and intuition. Many people have a preference, mine is left brain, hence writing a book with models, lists, facts. What's your preference? Notice when you get overly influenced by the facts and ignore your creativity or vice versa.

How to Balance

This isn't about letting go of your natural tendencies or preferences. It isn't about changing yourself. It isn't about going from one extreme to the other end of the continuum. As Dan Cable, a professor at London Business School, says, it's about having flexibility within a frame.[2] Define the landscape of how you want to be and what you want to create with other stakeholders and then play within that framework.

1. Know yourself and your usual responses or habitual tendencies (from Part 1).

2. Identify which tendencies are your growth opportunities. For example, if your tendency is to be task-led, your stretch zone would be how/relationship-led. Frame it as positive, what you want to practise, rather than what you want to avoid or not do.

3. Practise your growth opportunity with anyone anywhere. The "advanced program" would suggest practising your growth area with someone who is opposite to you or in a situation very much outside your comfort zone.

4. Notice the impact. Sense what effect you might be having on others. It's easy to say practise something that is a stretch for you. And how do you actually do that during your busy, potentially stressful, day? When we are stressed or time-pressured we tend to default to our old habits to ease the very pressure.

5. Practise when you can make some extra time, not when you're squeezed between two meetings. This could mean practising more during your personal time as you're standing on the side-lines of the rugby pitch with the other parents or with your kids. It's about practising while you are going about your normal life, not needing to create whole new episodes in an already busy schedule.

6. Carry around a visual reminder or structure of what you are trying to achieve – a picture on your journal/diary/phone or mug that depicts what you are trying to be or practise. An image or visual for what that balance is for you that you want to try to achieve.

7. Ask a trusted colleague, maybe an HR partner, for observations they have of you in meetings or interactions. Maybe they've heard comments about you at the water cooler that they can share.

THE CHALLENGE

Do the seven steps above in short:

1. Identify where you want to stretch yourself to have greater balance or more tools in your toolbox, more range in your responses as a leader.

2. Practise with safe people – those people that you trust and who trust you, such as friends, family, long-standing and respected work colleagues.

3. Notice the impact.

4. Refine your approach as needed – not because it feels uncomfortable, because it will feel uncomfortable. Try different things.

5. Repeat

After five days of playing or experimenting, sit down and reflect on the practice.

Reflect each time you do it:

- ▶ What did you learn about yourself from being more balanced? About others?

- ▶ What worked well? What do you need to still practise?

- ▶ What impact did you have? Either tangible (what people said to you about it) or intangible (what you feel/sense the impact was)?

- ▶ What are the differences between the various things you tried to balance?

- ▶ What have you noticed about other people's ranges? What works? What doesn't?

- ▶ What did you notice the first day versus the fifth, in terms of your ability/comfort?

Choose Courage And Vulnerability In Leadership (And Life)

This last Principle of Part 3 is certainly not the least. It's probably the foundation for all the previous Principles and, if I dare say it, your fulfilment and success in leadership, if not life! It's about putting yourself out there, trying new things, risking making a mistake or looking silly and feeling uncomfortable. Without embracing vulnerability and courage, the ideas in this book are just ideas and not opportunities; the challenges are just words and not possibilities for improving your work and life. My hope is that this section acts as your motivation to try something, anything, from the challenges and to keep trying.

Courage

Let's start with the *Oxford English Dictionary* definition of courage: "The ability to do something dangerous, or to face pain or opposition, without showing fear. Synonym: bravery."

So, it's not the absence of fear, it's the ability to move forward with something scary *despite* the fear! In terms of the office work environment few of us face real physical danger. Our courage is required less for dangerous situations and more for facing opposition, risk or fear of being judged. In fact, most people's biggest fear is being judged (by others as well as ourselves). Inc.com identified the five biggest fears bosses face every day and they all trace to judgement:[3]

1. Imposter syndrome, which is the fear of being found to be incompetent (this is the #1 fear among CEOs)

2. Looking stupid

3. Appearing vulnerable

4. Political attacks

5. Underachieving

As an Executive Coach I hear these insecurities often. "I am not good enough. I'm worried I appear weak or vulnerable. I am afraid of making a mistake or of being found out as not smart enough." Clients can share this with me as the coaching relationship is a safe, confidential space, and they often have few confidants with whom they'd risk revealing these fears or who would understand. I don't dismiss these fears, I get curious as to what's beneath them, so the client can empower themselves. I also reassure them about these fears using evidence such as the list above. Often, CEOs and MDs are surprised that their counterparts feel the same, that these feelings are normal; they thought it was exclusively their issue.

Courage or bravery is necessary at all levels of an organization. This is particularly true now, with all the uncertainty, volatility and increasing rate of change in the world. What worked yesterday might not work today and, even if it does, there may be a better way of working. Organizations need to innovate to stay relevant, which requires risk and potential failure. And let's face it, organizations themselves can't take risks; it's the people within those organizations that must innovate, take risks; in other words, be courageous.

There are two areas for applying courage in business:

1. Vocationally: The courage to do things differently, to have different solutions. This is about the work itself, changing a manufacturing or IT system, changing a process, using social media and paid product placement rather than traditional 30-second TV adverts. These changes feel less risky, easier to take, requiring less personal courage.

2. Personally: The courage to be different, to stand out, to go against the norm, to expose one's self. This is the courage to ask the 'stupid' question, to oppose the status quo, to put your head above the parapet about a decision or defined direction. This feels scary and risky, with huge repercussions to the individual.

There is a light side and a dark side to courage, as there is to every quality. The light side is powerful, brave, expanding, and the dark side is reckless, cavalier, and fool-hearted. The courage I'm espousing here is from the light side to increase your effectiveness, fulfil your potential and grow yourself on this journey of life. This is the courage that emotional intelligence and personal growth require.

As a coach I get these insecurities too. I sometimes bring things up in a coaching session that feel risky and I must call on my own courage. I usually design for this in our first coaching session when we design the alliance. In that initial session I ask the client if they want me to share any intuition that strikes me as we work together, and even though I've done that, it still feels scary in the moment, depending on what I'm sensing. And I try to phrase it in a way that is an inquiry or reflection rather than a pronouncement. In one small group coaching session, which is a shorter intervention so not as explicitly co-designed, I had a sense about a participant. He was talking about trust with his boss and I felt he wasn't trustworthy. What could I do with that? In the moment, I blurted out: "What might you be contributing to the distrust in the relationship?" Let's say it didn't land well. I got a lecture that coaches should be supporting not confronting. I felt a pang of shame; was worried about the impact on the other participants, that I hadn't got it 'right'.

On another occasion, I was doing a 1:1 session with a client, for which he was thoroughly prepared. He had decided he wanted to talk about his executive presence, as he was newly promoted to a senior position. As he was talking, I sensed something weighing on him. I asked about "any other topic that would be more important for you right now?" He said "no" and continued his train of thought. I interrupted and said, "I think there is, just can't put my finger on it. You're just ploughing through here." "Nope", he kept going. I held up a mirror to how he was being in the moment and asked, "What's going on?" and "Where else might this be happening in your life?" He didn't budge. My saboteurs were arriving – maybe I've got it wrong, who am I to say what we should work on, a better coach would nail it. So, I said something about his topic being 'presence' and he wasn't present, and my guess was that he wasn't at home and he was getting grief from his family. Silence. His eyes shifted upwards. (At this moment it's key as a coach to keep silent, let the client reflect and be with their thoughts.) He got very emotional and started talking about his family and the impact the new job was having on him and them – the topic that mattered most, not the vocational rather the personal. As he emailed me after the session, "The topic around my work life balance and family has been a big weight on my shoulders. I cannot stress enough just how much the session today helped me make sense of it all. I'm going home with light at the end of the tunnel."

Vulnerability

Vulnerability is defined by the *Oxford English Dictionary* as "the quality or state of being exposed to the possibility of being attacked or harmed, either physically or emotionally". At first glance this doesn't appear to be congruent with a leadership book and yet it is the basis for soft skills, emotional intelligence and authentic leadership.

No discussion of courage and vulnerability would be complete without homage to Brené Brown. If you haven't watched her TED talk on vulnerability, stop reading now and watch it (please come back to finish reading once you've watched it). She says that vulnerability is at the core or heart of meaningful human experiences. She has based this on her years of research as a Professor at the University of Houston and has shared it in her many bestselling books, *Daring*

Greatly and *Dare to Lead* being my two favourites.[4] She found that the block to being vulnerable was shame – the fear of not being worthy. Shame is about us feeling like we are a bad person, unworthy, flawed at our core. It can be confused with embarrassment or humiliation and yet it's not the same. Shame results from an individual reacting at an identity level to feedback (see Part 2 on where to take feedback) or what Brené calls 'self-talk': "How we experience these emotions comes down to self-talk. How we talk to ourselves about what's happening."[5] Shame self-talk is "I'm an awful person." Humiliation is the feeling of not deserving it: "That's not fair." Embarrassment is usually fleeting, situational and often funny: "Silly me, so typical."

Vulnerability is about exposing yourself, risking sharing something about yourself that might threaten your position or status. It's very different from being weak. Weakness is about lacking power to perform or having a flaw or limitation. Rob Goffee and Gareth Jones, in their book *Why Should Anyone Be Led By You?*, talk of allowable weaknesses as a means of showing vulnerability or authenticity.[6] A CEO could have an allowable weakness of public speaking which he's being supported to improve by a communication coach. However, he couldn't admit to 'not being good with numbers'. He can show a vulnerability to being self-conscious when giving a presentation. He can't show a fundamental deficit in doing his job. The former is revealing something about yourself that's personal or intimate whereas the latter is a comment about a shortcoming in your ability.

Last week I sensed a long-term client of mine wasn't saying something. We've been working together on his aspirations to become CEO. He's making great progress in terms of his leadership development and work responsibilities. I asked, "What aren't you saying?" His reply was "I guess this is where I can be vulnerable and share my fears." I reminded him of our contract of confidentiality and safety. He slowly revealed, more to himself than me, "Maybe I don't want to be a CEO." He was vulnerable to risk by admitting to himself that he might not want the dream he'd been doggedly pursuing for years and by exposing himself to all the consequences of that thought.

I have a personal example of vulnerability. I was on a first date and it seemed to be going really well. As we were sharing stories about ourselves, he choked up about a catastrophic skiing accident he'd had. He stopped talking to compose himself. I reached over and put my hand on his forearm to let him know he wasn't alone. As he tried to lighten the mood he asked about my parents in Canada and when I said they were dead the words caught in my throat and tears pooled in my eyes. Because he had been vulnerable with me, I felt vulnerable with him, my emotion just 'leaked' out unexpectedly.

Vulnerability requires trust of others and yourself. You need to trust the person with whom you are being vulnerable. You need to trust yourself that you have the courage to do it and can handle whatever happens following your revelation.

They Are Two Sides of the Same Coin

Courage and vulnerability are two sides of the same coin because you can't be vulnerable without being courageous and vice versa. It takes courage to risk being vulnerable, to reveal aspects of yourself that you've kept hidden/private or that might open you up to judgement or criticism or ridicule.

I hope you're seeing that vulnerability is anything but weak.

It's not about being vulnerable for vulnerability's sake. It's not about being vulnerable to manipulate someone. I'm suggesting that by being open to your vulnerability you can create greater connection with others, your stakeholders, at work and beyond. It's also about being yourself and feeling that you can show up fully at work, especially since we spend more of our waking hours at work than we do with friends and family. It's about creating an environment where others can be vulnerable too, with you role-modelling and creating that safe place. It's about creating a place where people can be courageous to dare, to risk exploring so that organizations innovate and create. You're the leader and the one reading this book, so you are the one to demonstrate living the two sides of the coin.

Cath's Case Study Example – Courage and Vulnerability

I coached a woman who worked in education, let's call her Cath, on and off for three years. She was a Deputy Head with a focus on special needs measures and wanted to be a Head Teacher. She had three challenges, all rooted in personal confidence: (i) she was unable to see her skills and where she added value; (ii) she struggled to sell herself in terms of instilling confidence in the interviewers and being clear in articulating her experience; and (iii) she found it a challenge to elevate herself from the detail of student issues and articulate a vision and strategy for the school as a whole. Let me be clear, she had the experience and ability, she simply needed to believe it.

We worked on various exercises for her internal belief and the external manifestation of that by preparing her for the interview process. She was beyond courageous, many times. On the first occasion she applied for a Head Teacher position, early in our coaching sessions, she talked exhaustively about individual student situations. The interview process required she supply a CV, and a written document of ideas for the school, and involved a 1:1 interview, followed by an intense panel interview. She didn't get the job. "It was gruelling", she said, disappointed yet relieved it was over. The feedback was honest and direct: "You have good experience and good ideas, but you don't come across like a Head Teacher." She was shaken. After some more work she again summoned up her courage and applied for another posting. She didn't get that one either. The feedback was improving, although they still commented: "You didn't seem very confident." The same thing happened several more times. On one occasion, she didn't even get on the shortlist for an interview.

She decided to take a sideways move to another Deputy post, "as I have been unsuccessful so many times in getting a post as a Head". This time it was for a 'challenging' school, way outside her experience and comfort zone. She got on with the job and started making a difference. She was approached by the governors in the summer about whether she'd be interested in the headship. Her initial reaction was "No" – "I swore I would never put myself through the gruelling process ever again. But the more I thought about it the more I came to realize that I was interested in the job. So, I decided to give it a go." Ah, plucky British courage.

"I had the interview this week – the whole process was as gruelling as I expected, but I have been offered the post. I wanted to say 'Thank you' for helping me on this road. You helped me have more confidence in myself, believe that I am good at what I do, and that I can make a difference. More importantly you helped me realize that I can be a good Head Teacher."

This is a wonderful example of courage, tenacity and vulnerability. She risked looking weak or incapable, faced constructive feedback, was rejected, felt she wasn't good enough. Yet she continued to put herself and her ideas in front of a scrutinizing audience in the pursuit of reaching her goal.

Living and operating from within your comfort zone will keep you feeling safe. On the other hand, new neural pathways are created when you step outside your comfort zone, into your stretch zone, by experimenting, practising and playing with different behaviours. Make it fun and see it as experimentation and you'll be able to relax your brain and make the change easier. Start with baby steps; the old saying 'How do you eat an elephant? One bite at a time' aptly applies here. It's not about changing everything at once, which pushes you into your chaotic zone which is overwhelming and unproductive. Take an iterative approach to your development, it's the journey of a lifetime.

As one client said, "One of the key learnings for me was that it's up to me to decide what I'm going to do: stay on the side-lines or take personal risks. Definitely without any hesitation, the stretch zone is so much more interesting, fun and intriguing than the comfort zone."

Comfort – Stretch – Chaotic Zones

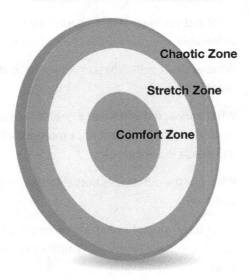

THE CHALLENGE

Where could you be more vulnerable? Think of the possibilities both at work and at home. Write down a list of at least 10 things.

Share two examples from your list this week. Start with something safe and small – maybe sharing how you feel if you don't normally do that, or where you feel insecure about something that's not central to your job or relationship.

Answer your why: Why do you want to try any of these challenges? What would it mean to you and your life to embrace these soft skills concepts? What motivated you to read this book? What is the reason that this might be important for you? Give your left brain something to do as your right brain works on the various challenges.

After sharing your two vulnerabilities, sit down and reflect on the practice.

Reflect each time you do it:

▶ What did you learn about yourself by being more vulnerable and courageous? About others?

▶ What worked well? What do you need to still practise?

▶ What impact did you have? Either tangible (what people said to you about it) or intangible (what you feel/sense the impact was)?

▶ What are the differences between the various things you tried?

▶ What have you noticed about other people's courage and vulnerability? What works? What doesn't?

▶ What did you notice the first day versus the fifth, in terms of your ability/comfort?

PART 4

BEYOND

This Part of the book started out as a bonus chapter until a few test readers said that this was the essence of my message and worthier than simply a tag-along bonus section. It transcends soft skills for more effective and fulfilling leadership and relationships. BEYOND is bigger than your work, your relationships and your skills. This is about the life you live and how you appreciate it.

Part 4 surrounds or underpins the first three Parts. Perhaps this is even the container that holds the first three elements of INSIDE, OUTSIDE AND BETWEEN. The operating system that runs the apps of your work and life. Sounds lofty – and it is. This is about life and death.

In fact, it will start with death. Death seems to have a way of bringing life into focus. Most people go to a funeral and then feel quite reflective afterwards of what that means for them. The same with a health scare, causing people to re-evaluate the time before the scare (or diagnosis) and the time after.

Then we will review life – with a suggestion of how to live it as a means of enjoying the journey and celebrating the big and small aspects of life.

PRINCIPLE 9

Live A Life Of No Regrets

This sounds slightly philosophical and it is my life purpose and a philosophy born out of real life and death experiences. Living a life of no regrets is the epitome of Soft Skills delivering Hard Results:

- You live your values and pursue a life of satisfaction in your uniquely 'you' way.

- You strive for 'clean' relationships – when things need to be said for another's benefit or for your emotional wellbeing, you have the conversation.

- You own your impact on other people and the world.

- You are courageous in your pursuits and relationships and therefore you're vulnerable.

- You balance all apparent contradictions and live with the paradoxes.

- You enjoy the journey, with one eye on creating the legacy you want.

- You realize every day could be your last.

My parents died unexpectedly 22 weeks apart. That changed my life. Their deaths led to my rebirth.

My Dad

Technically my father died from complications from
surgery for liver cancer – very clinical and science's
attempt to reach a logical, definitive conclusion,
something to write on a form so a file can be closed.
Medicine is not all science, it tries to be, and it is not.
Medicine can predict the plumbing, structural support
and electrical wiring of the body. Medicine cannot
account for will, spirit, or soul. My belief is that my Dad
died of a broken heart and fatigue. He was tired and sad
over the slow loss of his partner of 48 years – Mum was
still physically alive yet emotionally and intellectually
gone as she was succumbing to Alzheimer's for about
six years. Despite having survived colon cancer a few
years earlier and his oncologist saying that he could live
another five years with treatment post-surgery, I feel
my Dad lost hope and had no desire to continue living
what life had become. His spirit was empty, enjoyment
and meaning were gone. Now he was physically gone.

My Mum

In a routine white examination room in the same
hospital where Dad had died two months earlier, my
brother, Mum and I got the news that Mum had lung
cancer. She had a tumour the size of a grapefruit at
the top of her left lung. How could that be? She had
had chest x-rays done months earlier because she
had a cough and those x-rays showed nothing. The
doctor had no real explanation other than cancer can
advance quickly. I can still hear his words: "We can't
operate as it's big and near some major arteries. We
can't do radiation because it's so near the heart. And
chemo is not really an option as we have no idea how

chemo drugs impact someone with Alzheimer's. You need to treat it as palliative." With that he walked out the door. We just sat there, stunned. My brother and I stood up and embraced and then looked at my Mum; she stood up lost and confused, and started crying, I think because we were crying, I wasn't sure if she knew what this meant. The three of us embraced in a huddle almost hanging on for dear life and hope. We left the room, found a nurse and asked "Is that it? Do we just leave?" She checked with someone else and said yes, so the three of us walked down the corridor to the car park and headed home to figure out what next. For a few months Mum lived like she always had with my brother being her primary caregiver. We visited care homes to find one to move her to, as we had no idea how long she would live. On the day before I was to head back to Switzerland after a one-week visit (to be with my Mum and give my brother a well-deserved break) she was admitted to hospital with an apparent stroke. "Maybe the cancer had spread to her brain", they wondered. I stayed. For weeks we sat by her bedside. She was transferred to palliative care. A week before the sale of my parents' home was finalized, my Mum died. I believe she knew it was being sold and she didn't want to live without my Dad and outside of the home she loved.

My Rebirth

For about a year and a half after they died I lived in a fog of denial and suppression. I was on autopilot, going through the motions of life. I threw myself into work to make up for the time I had been away while both my parents were dying. Work became a good distraction. It was easy to not think about the loss as I was an ocean away and I had a good life by all accounts – I was married, living in Switzerland, working in a good job in a successful company, travelling for work and pleasure, socializing and having cool adventures. And I was empty.

I started grief therapy once I was able to be with the loss, I didn't feel so fragile that it would overwhelm me. I started to examine my feelings which were new for me. I realized that I was unhappy with a lot of my life. I had never seen or admitted that previously. Once the box of emotions was opened I couldn't close it again. I was doing a job because I was good at it even though I didn't like corporate politics and promoting consumerism. I was in a marriage that was lacking for me in emotional intimacy and safety. Having seen two people I loved draw their last breaths it became clear to me that life is finite; in my family of origin I was next in line in terms of mortality. And with my parents dead I had no fear of disappointing them with any subsequent decisions about my work or marriage. Their deaths created a clean slate from which I could create anything really. So, I did. I processed my grief. What did it mean to have no parents? I knew no one else in my age group who had lost both their parents and certainly not so close together. What was I feeling? What did I want more of in my life? How did I create or find what that is and then get it? I couldn't settle for OK with my one precious life. In a nutshell, after about two years of trying to improve our marriage we hit a roadblock over some historic issues that we couldn't navigate, and it was over. I left my big corporate job to start my own coaching business – to focus on individual impact and supporting others' personal growth as I had been supported. And I moved home and countries – going to the one that chose me. I'd never advise a client to change their work, relationship status and move at the same time. Amazingly, it worked for me.

I had been impacted to such a degree by the external circumstances of their deaths that I had to explore my new reality. Don't wait for an external event to reassess or change your life. Don't wait for a death of a loved one or a serious diagnosis for yourself or a loved one, a divorce or break-up of a relationship, to assess whether you are living the life you want to be living. Do it proactively and by motivation and choice rather than regret and reaction.

THE CHALLENGE

Think and feel your responses to the following questions:

What would you regret in life and at work if tomorrow your life ended? Or the life of your beloved?

If time and money were no object, what would you be doing with your life? What part of that, no matter how big or small, could you live now?

What legacy do you want to leave at work? At home? And in the world?

How do you bring some of the essence above to your everyday existence?

Take one small step towards something on the list above and do it today. One action.

Develop a plan this week for living a Life of No Regrets. That may seem lofty and, if not now, when?

Reflect each time you do it:

▸ What did you learn?

▸ What worked well? What do you need to still practise?

▸ What impact did living from the idea of a Life of No Regrets have on you? On others?

▸ What are the differences between a Life of No Regrets and your usual day?

▸ What have you noticed about other people's legacy?

▸ What did you notice the first day versus the fifth day of thinking about regrets and legacy?

PRINCIPLE 10

Live A Life Of Gratitude

I was a regular watcher of the *Oprah Winfrey Show* back in the 1990s–2000s. At that time, she was broadcasting her one-hour daytime talk show on national TV, well before she had her own network. In 1997 an episode of *Oprah* featured Sarah Ban Breathnach talking about her new book, *Simple Abundance: A Day Book of Comfort and Joy*.[1] I loved the show, so I bought the book and then its corresponding journal (which I dug out while writing this book to figure out the date I started my gratitude practice). I started the practice of capturing my daily gratitudes in that journal and have continued doing so on and off, but mostly on, for 22 years. It became a nightly practice and continues that way. It's a relaxing and peaceful way to end my day and go to bed to fall asleep.

Multiple research sources document the benefits of gratitude across five key areas:[2]

1. Emotional wellbeing – happier, less anxiety and depression, bounce back from stress

2. Physical health – better sleep, fewer aches and pains, less pain, more exercise

3. Personality – more optimism, self-esteem, spirituality

4. Social interactions – more friends, better marriages, deeper relationships

5. Career enhancements – greater networking, better teamwork, less absenteeism, greater employee and client loyalty

The Early Years

Initially it was hard to see what I was grateful for beyond the weather and something extra special, such as a gift, a work achievement or an acknowledgment. I'd get my journal out at night and struggle to write something, I'd almost feel like I was 'making it up'. I had to look back over the day and analyze my day to find the gratitude.

My early gratitudes from the first week of the practice were:

1. The neighbour's cat, Jack, visiting and purring while being petted

2. My patience in the return line at Ikea

3. It's Friday and I can sleep in tomorrow

After a while I started to look intentionally for things in my day that I could be grateful for because I knew I'd have to write something in my journal that night. Over time it evolved into me just noticing through the day 'oh, that's a gratitude' and now I see them many times through the day, it's just a natural observation and label for me.

These are some of my real gratitudes from today (the day I'm writing this section of the book):

1. Sharing laughs and venting frustrations with a group of female friends brought together by a mutual friend visiting London

2. Open, engaged clients willing to reflect and brainstorm how to be better in their organizations

3. A client sharing her experience of doing the gratitude practice (that's what motivated me to write this section today)

4. My local butcher agreeing to deliver my Christmas turkey to me the morning I need it, at no extra charge

5. An amazing dinner at one of my favourite restaurants, a vegetarian meal of complex flavours and textures

The Evolution

The practice started out just being what I was grateful for and then I added more to the practice as I evolved in my personal development journey. I added the following categories onto my nightly journaling:

- ME: I added something for which I was grateful or proud about myself. A self-gratitude so to speak. This is what I suggest to clients who have low self-confidence, doubt themselves or want a self-esteem boost.

- The BEST thing of the day, to really celebrate the highlight.

- The WORST of the day, to let go of it, without denying it, putting it in the past.

- The FEAR of the day, as I realized I was living from a place of fear a lot of the time, so I wanted to be more conscious about it and release it.

- The LEARNING of the day, to continue to learn and grow as I believe life and I are both a work in progress.

- One thing I was grateful for about MY PARTNER that day. Later I'd give him a page of gratitudes about him for the month and he started doing the same for me. I've since done it with boyfriends in their birthday or Christmas card and let's just say the British men are blown away by it!

These are examples of my extra gratitude categories from today:

Me: Asking a client if I can be extreme and provocative and then being that.

Best: A day that was satisfying across many aspects of my life – time with friends, fulfilling work, flavourful food, some lingering errands done, a potentially romantic introduction by a friend, my shoulder pain diminishing as I do my physio exercises.

Worst: The difficulty in writing the BEYOND section of my book; the most personal and original aspects of the book aren't flowing to really impart my strong desire for you to 'get this' material and live it!

Fear: This book not being any good and revealing personal aspects about myself in the book.

Learning: Looking at my thinking by asking "I notice that I'm having the thought that…" as a means of not making assumptions or getting hooked into counter-productive thoughts.

Some of my greatest gratitudes have been big and small moments of human interaction – which are just people skills borne out in daily life. It's the gobsmacked response of a fellow diner when I popped over to her table to tell her she looked beautifully pulled together – she blushed, stammered, excused the outfit as nothing special and when I softly said "receive the compliment" she did with a huge grin. It's working with a team of four highly successful partners yesterday about who they are when they are at their best and not having a dry eye in the session as they revealed themselves, acknowledged others and celebrated what makes each of them special. It's being told by a friend that I had hurt them with a comment and being able to resolve it between us. It's smiling at a stranger in the street and having them smile back.

Sara's Case Study Example – Gratitude Experience

A client, let's call her Sara, came to me knowing she was very critical of herself and wanting to feel more confident in her new job. While working together I asked her if she would like an exercise of self-appreciation. She said yes, so I explained the gratitude practice to her. Six weeks later, at the start of our next session, I asked her "What do you have to celebrate about yourself from the last six weeks? What qualities or characteristics of you are you proud of?" It's a question[3] I start all my coaching sessions with as it focuses people on their strengths rather than weaknesses or development areas (as we'll get to those in the bulk of the coaching session). She said she felt more positive, she had lifted the positivity of her team, inspired her MD to contribute more actively, and as a result they had won a new piece of business (the first in months). She reported feeling happier, more relaxed, grateful and positive, all tracing to the gratitude practice she had followed almost consistently since our previous coaching session.

Tips

- Physically write the gratitudes down in a journal or notepad – this engages your eyes, your hand (kinaesthetic movement), and your brain, making the gratitude more tangible as it's a multisensory exercise. If you only 'think' about them they are just more fleeting thoughts.

- Be specific – the detail is what makes the experience rich and creates the good feeling.

- Do it regularly, make it a habit.

- Do it for at least a month as the experience (and ease of doing it) will evolve over that time. It will get easier as you train your eye and brain to see the good in the moment.

- Find the time in the day that works best for you (ideally in the evening or night as you have your day to reflect on) and make the commitment to yourself to do it consistently.

THE CHALLENGE

Get a journal and every day for one month write five things you are grateful for from that day, then one thing about yourself for which you are proud, then the Best thing from the day, then the Worst thing from the day, a Fear from the day, and lastly something you learned today about yourself, life, living or the world.

You can download my gratitude worksheet/template from my website at www.directions-coaching.com/

It will look something like this each day:

1. Something I'm grateful for today

2. Another thing I'm grateful for today

3. Another thing I'm grateful for today

4. Again, another thing

5. You get the idea

Self: Something about yourself for which you are grateful or proud

Best: The best thing from the day

Worst: The worst thing from the day

Fear: A fear from the day

Learning: Something you learned today

Partner: Something about your partner you're grateful for

Bonus activity: Around the dining table ask your family or friends "What are you grateful for today?"

Reflect each time you do it:

▶   What did you learn?

▶   What worked well? What do you need to still practise?

▶   What impact did living from the idea of Gratitude have on you? On others?

▶   What are the differences between going through your day with Gratitude and your usual day?

▶   What have you noticed about other people's view or expression of Gratitude?

▶   What did you notice the first day versus the fifth day versus the thirtieth day of writing your daily gratitudes?

Soft Skills Hard Results Illustrative Model

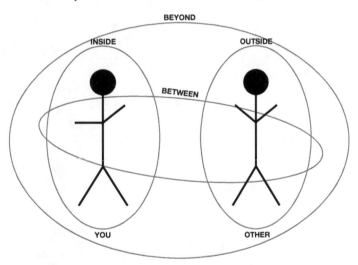

Final Note To Readers

I'm grateful that you're still reading, and I'm scared. Scared of your reaction. Scared of having made a mistake. Scared of not making a difference. Scared of things I can't even articulate right now. And I'm proud that I've actually risked putting this book and hence myself out into the world in service of those of you like me who aren't natural at soft skills.

I've tried to give you very practical examples for how to improve your people skills. I've only briefly explained why it's important, I hope enough to inspire you to pursue practising. If not, there are more publications in the bibliography to convince you. The journey of developing one's people skills is just that; recognize please that it's a journey and be compassionate with yourself as you are trying. I write about this because it's been my biggest development area in life, and I'm still practising.

There is a list of resources in the bibliography to support you in practising the elements in this book and to point you towards more in-depth resources as desired. There are worksheets on my website (www.directions-coaching.com) to support you in practising the exercises in the book – such as a template for how to give effective feedback and a tracking sheet for capturing your trials of all the ideas presented in the book.

People skills impact every area of our lives – professional and personal. People skills impact our enjoyment of life because few of us live a completely solitary life. I hope this is a precursor to further development for you around emotions and human interactions, hence emotional intelligence, and if you stop here that's OK too. There is no referee sitting on the side-lines of your life judging you as pass or fail. There is no end destination of perfection, rather it's about being in the game, living the journey of life. You're going to make mistakes, you're going to feel awkward, and the key is to stay in the game and keep learning. Strive to be your better self, except when you're not, so accept yourself at less than your best and recover to continue moving forward.

Contact, Coaching And Speaking

I've had various support systems over the years for learning and practising all these concepts. They include coaches, mentors, supervisors, therapists, trainers and friends. The journey of discovery and application is easier and deeper with a support system. If you'd like coaching support to work through this book or meet you where you're at in your leadership journey, please contact me at info@directions-coaching. com or LinkedIn. My DIRECT process of authentic leadership development starts with a complimentary call to assess if we have chemistry to work together, which on its own could result in transformation for you. I also conduct workshops and speaking engagements for work teams and groups on how to interact for increased productivity and fulfilment.

If you've had some learnings from this book and your associated practising, I'd love to hear about it. If you disagree with anything I've proposed, I'd love to hear about that too. The experience of learning and life is better shared. Feel free to share it with me.

Acknowledgements

Where to start? So many to name and I'm worried about missing someone.

I am deeply grateful for all the encouragement, support, inspiration and butt-kicking that has resulted in this book. Thank you.

The Practical Inspiration Publishing team of Alison Jones, Shell Cooper, Michelle Charman and Judith Wise. Alison – your process is genius and what you accomplish is unbelievable. My fellow bootcamp stayers of Angela, Celia and Grace. Thank you for being there in the beginning and helping make this a reality.

The people who first heard my 'leader quest' of writing a book and who continue to grow me as a leader and human – The Holly Tribe – Albert, Alex, Amber, Andreu, Bonnie, Caroline, Claire, Connor, Cynthia, Dorothee, George, Gizem, James, Judi, Kari, Louise, Nilgün, Otto, Rebecca, Regina, Saad, Sarah and Susie. And our initial leaders Rick and Jimena and assistants Claudia and Neil.

The Co-Active Training Institute (CTI). The coaches I've worked with and those I continue to work with as colleagues and learn from, especially the A&IWNESLG of Amanda, Louisa and Rona.

My numerous clients over the years who will remain nameless to maintain confidentiality. My coaches, mentors, supervisors, trainers and therapists who have worked with me to get me to a place of being brave enough to write this, vulnerable to going public, and helped me on my (continuing) development from head to heart.

The experts, influencers, teachers and inspirers I've been learning from for decades on this journey – many of whom are in the bibliography. Simon Achor, Justin Bariso, Travis Bradberry, Brené Brown, Les Brown, Dan Cable, Dale Carnegie, Susan Cain, Robert Dilts, Carol Dweck, Carmine Gallo, John Gray, Daniel Goleman, Jean Graves, Napoleon Hill, George Kohlreiser, Phil McGraw, Tom Peters, Tony Robbins, Sherly Sandberg, Robin Sharma, Simon Sinek, Captain Chelsy B. "Sully" Sullenberger III, Rick Tamlyn, Ruby Wax, Oprah Winfrey, Jack Wood.

The first people who read my manuscript, my test/beta readers, many of whom said they were honoured to have the opportunity (how lucky am I?) – Dan, David, Kathryn, Nilgün and Sean. And Laurie's help across the pond. Also, my first listener, Linda, and design support from Leigh.

My friends who are my family: Aneela, Darcie, Julie, Laura, Leigh, Lucy, Sarah, Steve and Sue. Thank you for your presence in my life.

Last but not least, my family. Mum and Dad, I miss you and you're always with me.

Notes

Note to Reader

[1] Travis Bradberry and Jean Greaves, *The Emotional Intelligence Quick Book: Everything You Need to Know to Put Your EQ to Work*. New York: Simon & Schuster, 2005, p.25.

[2] Daniel Goleman, *Emotion Intelligence: Why It Can Matter More Than IQ*. New York: Bantam Books, 1996.

[3] The business case for Emotional Intelligence 1999 by Consortium for Research on Emotional Intelligence in Organizations. http://www.eiconsortium.org/reports/business_case_for_ei.html

Introduction

[1] The business case for Emotional Intelligence 1999 by Consortium for Research on Emotional Intelligence in Organizations. http://www.eiconsortium.org/reports/business_case_for_ei.html

[2] Daniel Goleman, *Emotion Intelligence: Why It Can Matter More Than IQ*. New York: Bantam Books, 1996, p.26.

[3] BEabove Leadership 2014. https://www.beaboveleadership.com/

[4] Travis Bradberry and Jean Greaves, *The Emotional Intelligence Quick Book: Everything You Need to Know to Put Your EQ to Work*. New York: Simon & Schuster, 2005, p.6.

[5] BEabove Leadership 2014. https://www.beaboveleadership.com/

[6] 5 December 2010 https://www.psychologytoday.com/gb/blog/insight-therapy/201012/you-are-conformist-is-you-are-human

[7] Forbes, 4 August 2015 https://www.forbes.com/sites/victorlipman/2015/08/04/people-leave-managers-not-companies/#5cf1561647a9

Principle 1

[1] The Personal and Professional Identity Narrative (PPIN), Jack Denfeld Wood.

[2] Laura Whitworth, Karen Kimsey-House, Henry Kimsey-House, and Phillip Sandahl, *Co-Active Coaching: Changing Business, Transforming Lives: New Skills for Coaching People Toward Success in Work and Life.* London: Nicholas Brealey, 2007.

Principle 2

[1] Pia Mellody. http://www.piamellody.com/articles.html

[2] Louise Hay, *You Can Heal Your Life.* Carlsbad, CA: Hay House Inc., 2002, p.9. https://www.louisehay.com/about/

[3] https://www.psychologytoday.com/gb/blog/evolution-the-self/201606/you-only-get-more-what-you-resist-why

[4] https://www.psychologytoday.com/gb/blog/the-athletes-way/201705/diaphragmatic-breathing-exercises-and-your-vagus-nerve

Principle 3

[1] https://hbr.org/2013/03/the-ideal-praise-to-criticism

[2] Robert B. Dilts, *Next Generation Entrepreneurship: Success Factor Modeling, vol. I,* Scotts Valley, CA: Dilts Strategy Group, 2015, p.17.

Principle 4

[1] Laura Whitworth, Karen Kimsey-House, Henry Kimsey-House, and Phillip Sandahl, *Co-Active Coaching: Changing Business, Transforming Lives: New Skills for Coaching People Toward Success in Work and Life.* London: Nicholas Brealey, 2007, pp.34–40.

[2] John Whitmore, *Coaching for Performance.* London: Nicholas Brealey, 1992.

Principle 5

[1] https://alisonjones.com/

Part 3

[1] Stephen G. Gilligan and Robert Dilts, *The Hero's Journey.* Carmarthen: Crown House, 2009, p.29.

Principle 6

[1] Stephen R. Covey, *The 7 Habits of Highly Effective People.* New York: Simon & Schuster, 1990, p.235.

Principle 7

[1] BEabove Leadership and Uplift connect. https://upliftconnect.com/12-ways-unlock-powers-vagus-nerve/

[2] Daniel M. Cable, *Alive at Work.* Boston, MA: Harvard Business Review Press, 2018.

[3] 24 February 2015. Inc.com. Roger Jones, chief executive of London-based Vantage Hill Partners, study of 116 CEOs and other executives.

[4] Brené Brown, *Daring Greatly: How the Courage to be Vulnerable Transforms the Way We Live, Love, Parent, and Lead.* London: Penguin, 2012; Brené Brown, *Dare to lead.* London: Vermilion/Penguin, 2018.

[5] Brené Brown, *Daring Greatly*, p.71.

[6] Rob Goffee and Gareth Jones, *Why Should Anyone be Led by You?* Boston, MA: Harvard Business Review Press, 2006.

Principle 10

[1] Sarah Ban Breathnach, *Simple Abundance: A Day Book of Comfort and Joy.* Bantam, 1997.

[2] https://www.happierhuman.com/benefits-of-gratitude/; https://positivepsychologyprogram.com/benefits-gratitude-research-questions/

[3] Inspired by Dave Ellis, Coaching High Net Worth Clients Workshop. 2012.

Bibliography

21-Day Self-Confidence Challenge. Day Challenges, 2015. Print.

Achor, Shawn. *The Happiness Advantage.* London: Virgin, 2011. Print.

The Arbinger Institute. *Leadership and Self-Deception.* London: Penguin Books, 2007. Print.

The Arbinger Institute. *The Anatomy of Peace.* 2nd edn. Oakland: Berrett-Koehler Publishers Inc., 2015. Print.

'Are resumes passé? Enter the EQ test – Knowledge@ Wharton.' *Knowledge@Wharton.* 2014. 9 June 2019. Web.

Bariso, Justin. *EQ Applied.* Germany: Borough Hall, 2018. Print.

Bergland, Christopher. 'Diaphragmatic breathing exercises and your vagus nerve.' *Psychology Today.* 2017. 17 June 2019. Web.

Betz, Ann, and Ursula Pottinga. 'Be above leadership / The neuroscience of human transformation.' *Beaboveleadership.com.* 2019. 19 June 2019. Web.

Bradberry, Travis, and Jean Greaves. *Emotional Intelligence 2.0.* San Diego, CA: TalentSmart, 2009. Print.

Bradberry, Travis, and Jean Greaves. *The Emotional Intelligence Quick Book.* New York: Simon & Schuster, 2005. Print.

Breathnach, Sarah Ban. *Simple Abundance*. Bantam, 1997. Print.

Brown, Brené. *Dare to Lead*. London: Vermilion/ Penguin, 2018. Print.

Brown, Brené. *Daring Greatly: How the Courage to be Vulnerable Transforms the Way We Live, Love, Parent, and Lead*. London: Penguin, 2012. Print.

Cable, Daniel M. *Alive at Work*. Boston, MA: Harvard Business Review Press, 2018. Print.

Carnegie, Dale. *The Leader in You*. New York: Pocket Books, 1995. Print.

Cooper, Robert K., and Ayman Sawaf. *Executive EQ*. London: Texere, 2000. Print.

Covey, Stephen R. *Principle-Centered Leadership*. New York: Summit Books, 1990. Print.

Covey, Stephen R. *The 7 Habits of Highly Effective People*. New York: Simon & Schuster, 1990. Print.

Dent, Fiona, and Mike Brent. *Leader's Guide to Influence*. Pearson Education UK, 2010. Print.

Dilts, Robert B. *Next Generation Entrepreneurship: Success Factor Modeling, vol. I*. Scotts Valley, CA: Dilts Strategy Group, 2015. Print.

Duhigg, Charles. *The Power of Habit*. London: Random House Books, 2013. Print.

Dweck, Carol S. *Mindset*. London: Robinson, 2012. Print.

Ellis, David B. *Falling Awake*. Rapid City: Breakthrough Enterprises, Inc. 2002. Print.

Gallo, Carmine. *The Storyteller's Secret*. London: Macmillan, 2016. Print.

Gardner, Daniel. *The Science of Fear*. London: Plume, 2009. Print.

Gilligan, Stephen G., and Robert Dilts. *The Hero's Journey*. Carmarthen: Crown House, 2009. Print.

Goffee, Robert, and Gareth Jones. *Why Should Anyone be Led by You?* Boston: Harvard Business School Publishing, 2006. Print.

Goleman, Daniel. *Emotional Intelligence: Why it Can Matter More Than IQ*. London: Bloomsbury, 1996. Print.

Goulston, Mark, and Philip Goldberg. *Get Out of Your Own Way*. New York: Penguin, 1996. Print.

'Grow Model / Sir John Whitmore's Grow Coaching Model Framework.' https://www.performance consultants.com/grow-model. 10 June 2019. Web.

Hay, Louise. 'Autoimmune disease.' https://www. louisehay.com/natural-ways-treat-autoimmune-disease/ and https://www.louisehay.com/about/. 10 June 2019. Web.

Hay, Louise. *You Can Heal Your Life*. Carlsbad: Hay House Publishing, 2002. Print.

HBR's 10 MUST READS on Emotional Intelligence. Boston, MA: Harvard Business Press, 2015. Print.

Hendricks, Gay. *The Big Leap*. New York: HarperCollins, 2010. Print.

Jeffers, Susan J. *Feel the Fear and Do It Anyway*. London: Vermilion, 2012. Print.

Jennings, Marlene. 'From dis-ease to disease.' *Thriveglobal.com*. 2019. 10 June 2019. Web.

Jones, Roger. 'What CEOs are afraid of.' *Harvard Business Review*. 2015. 8 June 2019. Web.

Kimsey-House, Henry et al. *Co-Active Coaching*. 2nd edn. Mountain View: Davies-Black Publishing, 2007. Print.

Kline, Nancy. *Time to Think*. London: Ward Lock, 2004. Print.

Kohlrieser, George, and Joe W. Forehand. *Hostage at the Table*. San Francisco, CA: Jossey-Bass, 2006. Print.

Kohlrieser, George, Susan Goldsworthy, and Duncan Coombe. *Care to Dare*. Chichester: John Wiley & Sons, 2012. Print.

Lynn, Adele B. *The EQ Difference*. New York: Amacom, 2004. Print.

Mellody, Pia. 'Pia Mellody.' *Piamellody.com*. 2019. 19 June 2019. Web.

Palladino, Connie. *Developing Self-Esteem*. Menlo Park, CA: Crisp Publications, Inc., 1994. Print.

Robbins, Anthony. *Awaken the Giant Within*. New York: Fireside, 1992. Print.

Ruiz, Don Miguel. *The Four Agreements*. San Rafael, CA: Amber-Allen Publishing, 1997. Print.

Sandberg, Sheryl. *Lean In*. Croydon: Random House UK, 2015. Print.

Seligman, Martin E. P. *Learned Optimism*. New York: Pocket Books, 1990. Print.

Seltzer, Leon F. 'You only get more of what you resist –
why?' *Psychology Today*. 2016. 9 June 2019. Web.

Tamlyn, Rick. *Play Your Bigger Game*. London: Hay
House Publishing, 2013. Print.

Wax, Ruby. *How To Be Human*. London: Penguin Life,
2018. Print.

Wax, Ruby. *Sane New World*. London: Hodder &
Stoughton Ltd, 2014. Print.

Whitmore, John. *Coaching for Performance*. London:
Nicholas Brealey, 1992. Print.

Wood, Jack Denfeld. 'The Personal and Professional
Identity Narrative (PPIN).' Unpublished.

'You are a conformist (that is, you are human).'
Psychology Today. 2005. 13 July 2019.Web.

Zenger, Jack, and Joseph Folkman. 'The ideal praise-to-
criticism ratio.' *Harvard Business Review*. 2013. 17 June
2019. Web.